Neurofeedback - The Neurofeedback Book for Patients and Therapists : A Symphony of the Mind

Jean-Maurice Cecilia-Menzel

Published by Jean-Maurice Cecilia-Menzel, 2022.

NEUROFEEDBACK - THE NEUROFEEDBACK BOOK FOR PATIENTS AND THERAPISTS : A SYMPHONY OF THE MIND

First edition. October 24, 2022.

ISBN: 979-8215496343

Written by Jean-Maurice Cecilia-Menzel.

Jean-Maurice Cecilia-Menzel

Medical practitioner for psychotherapy

Hildeboldstrasse 1, 80797, Munich, Germany

telephone: 089 44135911

e-mail: info@neurofeedback-praxis-muenchen.de

Competent supervisory authority:

Public Health Office Munich

Professional liability insurance with

Hiscox SA, Branch Office for Germany

Chief representative: Robert Dietrich

Arnulfstrasse 31

80636 Munich

Tel.: +49 89 54 58 01 281

Responsible tax office

Tax office Munich

Table of Contents

What is neurofeedback?

Overview

Neurofeedback is a form of biofeedback, characterized by the ability to consciously control the brain waves. During neurofeedback therapy, the brain waves are recorded using electroencephalography (EEG). The components of the EEG are extracted and demonstrated to the therapy recipients as audio, video, or both. During neurofeedback therapy, therapy recipients are capable of assessing the changes and their progress for optimum treatment performance. The recipients tend to improve their brain patterns in response to the assessed changes. (Marzbani et al., 2016)

Neurofeedback treatment protocols comprise alpha, gamma, theta, delta, and beta treatment. The treatment protocols may also include a combination of these components, such as beta/theta ratio and alpha/theta ratio. Frequently used treatment protocols include alpha/theta ratio, alpha, theta, and beta treatment. Subsequent subsections will discuss the different aspects of neurofeedback training.

Frequency Components

Activated neurons produce electrical pulses, attributing to the electrical activity of the brain. EEG involves the placement of electrodes over the scalp, to record the electrical activity of the brain. In particular, EEG measures the synchronous electrical activity of the pyramidal neurons of the brain which reflect onto the overlying skin, corresponding to the electrodes placed on the scalp. The brain waves, or patterns of electrical activity, have distinct frequencies and amplitudes. The frequency of the brain waves determines the speed of oscillation of brain waves, indicated by the number of waves each second - hertz (Hz). The amplitude of the brain waves is indicated by microvolt (μV). Frequency components of the brain waves represent a specific physiological function and include the following.

Delta waves (< 4 Hz) are observed when an individual is asleep.

Theta waves (4-8 Hz) are observed when an individual is sleepy or drowsy.

Alpha waves (8-13 Hz) are observed when an individual is awake, relaxed, and the muscles are loose.

Beta waves (13-30 Hz) are observed when an individual is alert.

Gamma waves (30-100 Hz) are observed when an individual is awake and solving a problem.

The frequency components are further divided into subsets. Low beta, also known as sensorimotor rhythm (SMR) frequency bands, corresponding to the sensorimotor rhythm with a frequency range of 13-15 Hz. While some studies demonstrate two subsets of alpha waves, others describe three subsets of alpha waves. In contrast to the higher alpha wave, the lower-alpha wave is associated with semantic memory. (Schönenberg et al., 2017)

Types of Neurofeedback Training

Following are the different types of neurofeedback training, employed for the treatment of different disorders.

Frequency/power neurofeedback is the most prevalent form of neurofeedback training. This type of neurofeedback uses 2-4 surface electrodes. Therefore, it is also called surface neurofeedback. This is used for the treatment of anxiety, insomnia, and attention deficit hyperactivity disorder (ADHD).

Slow cortical potential neurofeedback (SCP-NF) is used for the treatment of migraines, ADHD, and epilepsy. This type of neurofeedback training influences the direction of SCP in the brain.

Low-energy neurofeedback system (LENS) is used for the treatment of restless leg syndrome, ADHD, anxiety, depression, traumatic brain injury, anger, insomnia, and fibromyalgia. LENS employs weak electromagnetic signals while the treatment recipient remains motionless with eyes closed so that the recipients can change their brain waves.

Hemoencephalographic (HEG) neurofeedback training is used for the treatment of migraines. It involves cerebral blood flow feedback.

Live Z-score neurofeedback training provides continuous feedback by a continuous comparison between the systemic database and brain electrical activity variables. This neurofeedback training helps treat insomnia.

Low-resolution electromagnetic tomography (LORE-TA) uses 19 electrodes for monitoring the coherence, phase, and power. LORE-TA is used for the treatment of the obsessive-compulsive disorder (OCD), addictions, and depression.

The most recent form of neurofeedback training, functional magnetic resonance imaging (fMRI), regulates the activity of the brain based onck received from deep subcortical regions.

Placement of EEG Electrodes

EEG electrodes are placed on the scalp to monitor the electrical activity of the brain. The Electrode System 10-20 standardizes the areas of the skull and compares the obtained data. "10-20" indicates the electrode placement on 10% or 20% of the total area between the skull locations. The placement of electrodes corresponds to the cerebral cortical areas. While 2 electrodes function as reference electrodes, the other 19 electrodes record the electrical activity of the cortical areas.

The letters indicate the brain regions F (frontal area), P (parietal area), T (temporal area), O (occipital area), and C (central area). The numbers (odd and even) are associated with the right and left hemispheres of the brain. P_z corresponds to the location of electrodes along the central line, between inion and nasion. F_{P1} and F_{P2} indicate left and right forehead poles, respectively. A1 and A2 are related to the left and right vestibular or ear regions. A1 and A2 are common sites for ground and reference electrode placement.

Neurofeedback training may involve unipolar or bipolar modes of electrode placement. In the unipolar montage, the active electrode, placed on the skull, records brain electrical signals that are compared to the second or reference electrode. The brain activity is determined by subtracting the reference electrode activity from the active electrode activity. The bipolar montage involves the placement of two active electrodes on the skull. The brain activity during the neurofeedback training is determined by the difference in signals recorded by the two active electrodes. (Enriquez-Geppert et al., 2019)

The related EEG channel is present on one side of the brain. The training of beta and low beta components occurs on the left (C_3) and right (C_4) sides of the brain, respectively. Opposite placement of the electrodes such as low beta training on the left side may lead to mental energy depletion, which would have improved concentration if placed correctly. Hence, it is important to place the EEG electrodes in the correct location during neurofeedback training.

Elements of Neurofeedback Training

The neurofeedback training is based on either high or low frequencies. Low frequencies, including alpha and theta waves, are effective for improving focus and strengthening relaxation. On the contrary, high frequencies, theta, beta, and low beta waves; are associated with organizing, inhibiting distractibility, and reinforcing activation. For low-frequency neurofeedback training, eyes are closed and only adults receive the training. In contrast to this, high-frequency neurofeedback training requires the opening of the eyes and can be administered to both adults and children. (Fox et al., 2005)

Treatment Protocols

Following are the different treatment protocols of neurofeedback training.

Alpha Protocol

Alpha waves of the brain are related to alert relaxation and represent a calm and pleasant mood. The alpha waves exhibit creativity, associated with the state of relaxation. As alpha waves occur in the brain, the muscles relax. Meditation tends to increase the activity of alpha waves in the brain. At specific frequencies, the alpha waves are effective for the following disorders.

9 Hz stimulation for pain relief

10 and 30 Hz stimulation for alleviating stress and anxiety

10.2 Hz stimulation for treating brain injuries and improving memory and mental performance

7-10 Hz is the most common frequency bandwidth used in the alpha protocol of neurofeedback training. This frequency range is associated with sleep, alleviation of stress and anxiety, and meditation. 10 Hz stimulation is used in deep muscle relaxation, regulating the rate of breathing, pain reduction, and heart rate reduction. (Gruzelier, 2008)

Beta Protocol

Beta waves of the brain represent mental performance. Inappropriate beta activity is indicative of physical and mental disorders that include ADHD, insomnia, and depression. Beta activity is associated with problem-solving abilities, conscious precision, and strong focus. At specific frequencies, the beta training is effective for the following functions.

12-14 Hz stimulation for improving attention and focus

7-9 Hz stimulation for improving the reading ability

14-22 Hz and 12-15 Hz stimulation for overthinking, OCD, cognitive processing, excessive worries, alcoholism, insomnia, and computational performance.

12-15 Hz stimulation for the reduction of stress, anxiety, anger, and epilepsy.

Beta training with relevant light and sound also improves the sleep cognitive performance while alleviating stress and fatigue. (Gruzelier, 2008)

Alpha/Theta Protocol

Alpha/theta activity of the brain represents the distinction between sleep and awareness. This protocol of neurofeedback training is well known for its role in reducing stress. This form of neurofeedback training is also associated with addiction, depression, relaxation, anxiety, musical performance, trauma-related healing, and creativity. The frequency bandwidth for alpha/theta training is 7-8.5 Hz. During the treatment, auditory feedback is used while the therapy recipient keeps their eyes closed.

Delta Protocol

The delta waves are observed in the third and fourth stages of sleep. These are the slowest brain waves and represent sleep, reduce pain, and increased comfort. Delta waves are used for the treatment of learning disorders, hard and sharp muscle contractions, headaches, and traumatic brain injury via 1-3 Hz stimulation. The delta waves eliminate worries or concerns as well as improve sleep. (Reis et al., 2016)

Gamma Protocol

Gamma waves are the highest frequency brain waves and are associated with memory and cognitive processing. Faster gamma waves are related to a faster speed of recalling memory. These fast rhythms determine the transfer of data from the brain to the outside world. Gamma waves are present in the hippocampus of the brain, which is responsible for the conversion of short-term memory to long-term memory. Gamma waves are also observed in spasms, seizures, and other sudden attacks. Gamma protocol in neurofeedback training is essential for problem-solving skills, mental sharpness, cognition, and brain activity. Gamma training reduces the frequency of migraines attacks and increases information processing speed.

Theta Protocol

Theta waves of the brain are associated with emotion, sleep, memory, hypnosis, creativity, and meditation. The first stage of sleep also exhibits theta waves. Neurofeedback training with theta protocol is effective for the treatment of emotional disorders, ADHD, daydreaming, anxiety, depression, and distractibility.

Clinical Applications

Abnormal structural and physiological attributes of the brain are associated with poor mental performance and impaired quality of life. Neurofeedback training is pivotal to the treatment of various disorders and diseases that are described as follows.

Attention Deficit Hyperactivity Disorder (ADHD)

ADHD is associated with the malfunctioning of the frontal lobe of the brain. ADHD symptoms include distractibility, hyperactivity, and inattention. The aim of neurofeedback training is to restore the normal behaviors in ADHD patients, without relying on pharmacological formulations or behavioral therapy. Medications for ADHD are not clinically effective and are associated with adverse effects such as decreased appetite, abdominal pain, headache, insomnia, anxiety, and irritability. When compared to healthy subjects, individuals with ADHD tend to have slower activity of beta and theta brain waves.

The goal of neurofeedback training is to lower the theta brain activity and increase beta activity in the brain. In other words, neurofeedback training aims to decrease the theta/beta ratio at the electrode.

Neurofeedback training reduces hyperactivity and improves focus and sustained attention in ADHD patients.

Schizophrenia

Individuals suffering from schizophrenia experience illusions of restlessness, delirium, confusion, depression, auditory disorders, and non-flexible muscles. Schizophrenia patients who receive neurofeedback training become capable of adjusting their brain activity according to certain frequencies.

Insomnia

Insomnia is an epidemic sleeping disorder. Neurofeedback training in insomnia patients improves sleep patterns of insomnia patients and improves the quality of sleep. With neurofeedback training, individuals can sleep faster. Following are the two processes involved in neurofeedback training for sleep disorders.

Neurofeedback training is performed for 30 minutes at 15-18 Hz frequency, using a single electrode. This method of neurofeedback training assists the therapy recipients in waking up faster.

Calmness treatment is performed at a frequency range of 12-15 Hz.

Learning Disabilities

Neurofeedback training is an effective therapeutic measure for learning disabilities such as dyscalculia and dyslexia. Dyslexia patients have difficulties in spelling and reading, whereas individuals with dyscalculia face challenges related to math problems. Neurofeedback training increases the activity of alpha waves in the brain.

Drug Addiction

Neurofeedback training plays an important role in overcoming drug addiction while reducing the craving and temptation of drugs. Neurofeedback training is an effective therapeutic measure for alcoholism, computer games addiction, and cocaine addiction.

Enhanced Professional Performance

Professional athletes, surgeons, and artists demonstrate distinct brain activity patterns. Neurofeedback training employs these brain patterns to enhance professional performance in relatively unprofessional individuals. Neurofeedback training in professional athletes improves their psychomotor ability, self-regulation ability, confidence, and performance.

Autistic Spectrum Disorder (ASD)

ASD is referred to as a neurodevelopmental disorder, the symptoms, and challenges, of which persist through adulthood. Children diagnosed with ASD face difficulties in verbal communication, non-verbal communication, interests, behavior, and social interaction. ASD is also associated with mental retardation, seizure disorders, and emotional problems. Autistic children develop extreme sensitivity to smells and sound as well as demonstrate poor social interaction, obsessive rumination, and idiosyncratic behavior. The diagnostic characteristics of ASD include high beta activity associated with anxiety; high delta/theta activity associated with impulsivity, hyperactivity, and lack of attention; and seizure activity. Approximately 50-60% of ASD patients demonstrate high beta activity. Neurofeedback training for ASD patients enhances the beta wave activity and inhibits the theta/alpha ratio. (Domingos et al., 2021)

Epilepsy

Epilepsy-specific medications are clinically ineffective in a significant percentage of epilepsy patients. Effective treatment for such patients is neurofeedback training. Reduced slow rhythms with a frequency range of 4-7 Hz and increased SMR with a frequency range of 12-15 Hz are diagnostic characteristics of epilepsy. Continuous SMR treatment in epilepsy patients modulates uncontrolled epilepsy and lowers the rate of seizures.

Depression

Depression is characterized by hypometabolism in different regions of the brain including the cingulate, insula, anterior temporal cortices, frontal cortex, thalamus, amygdala, and basal ganglia. Depression patients without significant anxiety demonstrate decreased activation of the right parietal lobe. Neurofeedback training alleviates depression by suppressing faster beta waves while increasing the activity of the alpha and theta waves.

Anxiety

Anxiety is characterized by increased muscle tension. Since anxiety is associated with the inhibition of alpha waves, alpha wave neurofeedback training may alleviate anxiety. Moreover, electromyogram (EMG) biofeedback for both specific and generalized patterns of anxiety.

Pain Management

Pain is a symptomatic manifestation of physical injury. Neurofeedback training equips an individual with self-regulation of the pain. Therefore, the therapy recipient can reduce and eliminate the sensation of pain. Chronic pain patients have altered functional organizations in the somatosensory cortex of the brain. Neurofeedback training is integral to pain management as it influences pain perception processing.

Conclusion

Neurofeedback training enables the therapy recipients to control their brain activity. The brain activity is assessed using EEG and the extracted information is fed to the therapy recipient for modifying and regulating the brain activity. The neurofeedback training involves the placement of electrodes on appropriate regions of the scalp. Based on the quantity and placement of electrodes, neurofeedback training is categorized into a unipolar and bipolar montage. Neurofeedback training includes alpha, gamma, delta, beta, theta, and alpha/theta protocols. These protocols are based on the specific frequency components of neurofeedback training, which correspond to certain physiological states of the brain. Neurofeedback training has numerous clinical applications such as the treatment of learning disorders, ASD, ADHD, anxiety, depression, epilepsy, pain management, drug addiction, schizophrenia, and insomnia.

Tasks of the brain

Brief Introduction to Brain Anatomy

The human brain is grossly divided into the cerebrum, cerebellum, and brain stem. The cerebellum is divided into right and left hemispheres. The cerebral hemispheres are characterized by surface convolutions, gyri, sulci, and fissures. The cerebral hemispheres have an inner core of the white matter and an outer layer of grey matter, which is termed the cerebral cortex. The cerebral cortex is further divided into frontal, temporal, occipital, and parietal lobes. The cerebellum is composed of deep cerebellar nuclei and outer grey matter, known as the cerebellar cortex. The cerebellar cortex comprises granular, Purkinje, and molecular layers. The cerebellar peduncles connect the cerebellum with different parts of the brain stem. The cerebellum is responsible for maintaining posture, balance, and coordinating motor activities. The brain stem is located between the spinal cord and at the base of the cerebrum. The brain stem consists of the medulla, pons, and midbrain. (Herbet & Duffau, 2020)

Functions of Frontal Lobe

The frontal lobe is the largest lobe of the brain, which is located anterior to the cerebral hemispheres. The frontal lobe is responsible for speech, prospective memory, and language. Broca's area of the frontal lobe is involved in the production of speech. The frontal lobe is associated with the personality attributes of an individual. Damage to the frontal lobe and prefrontal cortex may stimulate different types of personality changes such as executive disturbances, distress, decision-making, disturbed social behavior, hypo-emotionality, and emotional dysregulation. The PROBE model describes the role of the frontal lobe in the decision-making process and adaptation to certain situations or circumstances. The motor cortex in the frontal lobe of the brain is divided into the primary motor areas and non-primary motor areas, including the cingulate motor area, premotor cortex, and supplementary motor area. Lesions of the frontal lobe present with weakness, flaccid hemiplegia, aphasia, apraxia, and personality disorders.

Functions of Parietal Lobe

The parietal lobe of the brain is located superior and posterior to the temporal and frontal lobes, respectively. The two functional regions of the parietal lobe include the anterior parietal lobe and posterior parietal lobe. The anterior parietal lobe comprises the primary sensory cortex. This receives sensory information relayed from the thalamus and interprets this information. The anterior parietal lobe processes simple somatosensory signals that include touch, pressure, pain, vibration, temperature, and position. The posterior parietal lobe comprises the superior parietal lobule and inferior parietal lobule. The former includes the somatosensory association cortex that is associated with motor planning action and other higher-order functions. The inferior parietal lobule contains the secondary somatosensory cortex. Two characteristic components of the inferior parietal lobule are the supramarginal gyrus and angular gyrus. This region receives somatosensory information from the thalamus and contralateral secondary somatosensory cortex and integrates this information with visual inputs, auditory inputs, and other modalities. Functions of the inferior parietal lobule include learning, language, spatial recognition, sensorimotor planning, and stereognosis. Stereognosis refers to the ability to distinguish between objects because of their shape, weight, size, and other attributes. Lesions of the parietal lobe manifest as loss of sensation, aphasia, apraxia, and astereognosis. (Choo et al., 2020)

Functions of Occipital Lobe

The occipital lobe is present in the posterior-most region of the brain. This is the smallest lobe and is located posterior to both the temporal and parietal lobes of the brain. The occipital lobe is responsible for the processing and interpretation of visual information. The primary visual cortex in the occipital love receives visual input relayed from the thalamus. The occipital lobe interprets the visual information and sends this information to other regions of the brain, such as the inferior temporal lobe. Lesions of the occipital lobe manifest as visual deficits, including color blindness or complete blindness. (Choo et al., 2020)

Functions of Temporal Lobe

The temporal lobe of the brain is located posterior and inferior to the frontal and parietal lobes, respectively. The temporal lobe has a lateral and a medial surface. The lateral surface of the temporal lobe is characterized by the lateral temporal sulcus and superior temporal sulcus. These sulci divide the lateral surface of the temporal lobe into superior, middle, and inferior temporal gyri. The lateral surface of the temporal gyrus comprises the Wernicke's area, which was previously known to be associated with comprehension and perception of speech. The superior temporal gyrus comprises the secondary auditory cortex, which is responsible for the interpretation of sounds. The middle temporal gyrus is associated with semantic memory and semantic control of different brain regions. The inferior temporal gyrus comprises the ventral visual pathway and is responsible for visual and facial perception. The medial surface of the temporal lobe is associated with the hippocampus, entorhinal cortex, parahippocampal cortex, and perirhinal cortex. This brain region is responsible for declarative memory, which is further divided into semantic memory, recognition memory, episodic memory, recollection, and familiarity. Lesions of the temporal lobe manifest as deafness, phenomic paraphasia, and hallucinations (auditory, memory, and visual).

Functions of Brainstem

The brainstem is a bridge between the cerebrum, cerebellum, and spinal cord. From superior to inferior, the components of the brainstem include the following structures.

Diencephalon

Midbrain

Pons

Medulla Oblongata

The brainstem performs the vital functions of life, which include breathing, blood pressure, heart rate, sleep, and consciousness. Grey matter comprises brainstem nuclei, and white matter attributes to the tracts of the brain stem. The brainstem also gives rise to 10 cranial nerves.

The diencephalon connects to the cerebrum superiorly and midbrain inferiorly. The diencephalon surrounds the third ventricle and comprises the thalamus, epithalamus, subthalamus, and hypothalamus. Epithalamus is composed of the posterior commissure, habenular commissure, and pineal gland. The subthalamus is a superior extension of the midbrain tegmentum and comprises the red nucleus, substantia nigra, and subthalamic nucleus. The hypothalamus consists of the infundibulum, hypophysis, hypothalamic nuclei, and mammillary bodies. The thalamus flanks the third ventricle and relays the sensory input to relevant brain areas. (Choo et al., 2020)

The midbrain is present between pons and diencephalon. It consists of a cerebral aqueduct, which connects the third and fourth ventricles. Superior colliculi of the midbrain participate in visual reflexes, including saccadic eye movements. The inferior colliculi are responsible for the processing of auditory information. The midbrain also comprises substantia nigra, red nucleus, and dorsal raphe nucleus. Substantia nigra, with basal ganglia, regulates motor activities. The red nucleus is also associated with movements and is connected to the cerebellum. The medial longitudinal fasciculus of the midbrain plays an important role in the coordination of eye movements.

Pons is located between the medulla oblongata and midbrain. Pons is associated with the basilar artery anteriorly and the fourth ventricle posteriorly. Pons comprise locus coeruleus, pointing nuclei, and cranial nerve nuclei. Locus coeruleus produces norepinephrine and is associated with the reticular activating system. Pontine nuclei are responsible for the coordination of movements and regulation of breathing.

The medulla oblongata is the connection between the pons and spinal cord. Anteriorly, the medulla oblongata comprises pyramids, which are collections of motor fibers from the motor cortex to the spinal cord, subsequently controlling the contraction of muscles. Gracile and cuneate nuclei of the medulla oblongata are involved in the relay of sensory information to the higher centers. (Ackerman, 2022)

Functions of Cerebellum

The cerebellum is located posterior to the cerebral cortex and underlies the temporal and occipital lobes of the brain. The cerebellum comprises 50% of the neurons and 10% of the total brain volume. Although the cerebellum does not generate motor commands, it functions to modify the motor signals carried by the descending tracts to modulate the accuracy and precision of the movements. Following are the important functions of the cerebellum. (Ackerman, 2022)

The cerebellum is responsible for the maintenance of balance and posture. It compensates for the changes in body position or muscle load to modulate motor movements. Hence, cerebellar damage may manifest as balance disorders.

The cerebellum facilitates coordination of the force and timing of voluntary movements to produce smooth body or limb movements.

The cerebellum is also responsible for motor learning. It is an integral component of fine-tuning and adapting motor programs that perform accurate movements with the trial-and-error mechanism.

The cerebellum is also involved in cognitive functions, including language.

Conclusion

The human brain is grossly divided into the frontal lobe, parietal lobe, temporal lobe, occipital lobe, cerebellum, and brainstem, with each structure having distinct anatomical and physiological characteristics. The frontal lobe is the largest lobe of the brain and is associated with prospective memory, language, and speech. The frontal lobe is also responsible for the control of the behavior and personality of an individual. Posterior to the frontal lobe is the parietal lobe, which is further divided into the anterior and the posterior parietal lobes. While the anterior parietal lobe contains the primary association cortex, the posterior lobe comprises the secondary somatosensory cortex and somatosensory association cortex. The parietal lobe is responsible for learning, language, spatial recognition, sensorimotor planning, and stereognosis. The occipital lobe is the smallest and posterior-most lobe of the brain. The occipital lobe is responsible for the processing and interpretation of visual information. The temporal lobe is located inferior and posterior to the parietal and frontal lobes, respectively. It is responsible for declarative memory and auditory processing. The brain stem connects the cerebrum, cerebellum, and spinal cord. It gives rise to cranial nerves and comprises the diencephalon, medulla oblongata, midbrain, and pons. The midbrain comprises superior and inferior colliculi that are responsible for visual and auditory information processing. Pons is associated with the coordination of movements, and regulation of breathing, and comprise the reticular activating system. Medulla oblongata regulates vital body functions and consists of the motor and sensory tracts. The cerebellum is associated with the regulation and coordination of motor movements, maintenance of balance and posture, motor learning, and cognitive functions.

Structure and organization of the brain

Introduction to Anatomy of the Brain

The human brain is grossly divided into the cerebrum, cerebellum, and brain stem. The cerebellum is divided into right and left hemispheres. The cerebral hemispheres are characterized by surface convolutions, gyri, sulci, and fissures. The cerebral hemispheres have an inner core of white matter and an outer layer of grey matter, which is termed the cerebral cortex. The cerebral cortex is further divided into frontal, temporal, occipital, and parietal lobes.

Lobes of the Brain

Parietal Lobe

The parietal lobe is present inferior, posterior, superior, and anterior to the parietal bone, frontal lobe, temporal lobe, and occipital lobe respectively. The central sulcus demarcates the anterior border of the parietal lobe. The posterior border of the parietal lobe is not well-defined. It is characterized by an imaginary line, which extends between the preoccipital notch inferiorly and the parietooccipital sulcus superiorly. The lateral sulcus or Sylvian fissure forms the inferior border of the parietal lobe, whereas the superior border is made by the medial longitudinal fissures that are present between the two cerebral hemispheres.

The parietal lobe is composed of three distinct regions - postcentral gyrus, superior parietal lobule, and inferior parietal lobule. The postcentral gyrus corresponds to the primary somatosensory cortex (BA 1, 2, and 3) and runs parallel to the central sulcus. The postcentral gyrus received sensory information relayed from the spinothalamic pathway (temperature and pain) and dorsal column pathway (fine touch, vibration, and proprioception). Superior and inferior parietal lobules of the posterior portion of the parietal lobule are separated by the intraparietal sulcus. The superior parietal lobule integrates the sensorimotor information, and the inferior parietal lobule is responsible for language and auditory functions. (Ackerman, 2022)

Frontal Lobe

Three cortical surfaces of the frontal lobe include inferior, lateral, and medial surfaces. The lateral surface comprises the precentral, middle frontal, inferior frontal, and superior frontal gyri. The medial or interhemispheric surface of the frontal lobe comprises the paracentral lobule and superior frontal gyrus. The inferior surface of the frontal lobe comprises the orbital gyri, olfactory bulb, and olfactory tract.

The frontal cortex is composed of three parts - Broca's area, prefrontal cortex, and motor cortex. The prefrontal cortex includes the frontal lobe gyri (superior, middle, and inferior). It is responsible for emotional and intellectual processing, decision-making, and judgment. The motor cortex corresponds to the precentral gyrus and is composed of the primary motor cortex (BA 4). The motor cortex integrates information from different areas of the brain in order to modulate motor functions. The primary motor cortex gives rise to the corticospinal tract. The premotor area or premotor cortex and supplementary motor cortex are located anterior to the primary motor cortex. These two areas organize the actions and movements of the body. The inferior and middle frontal gyri comprise frontal eye fields (BA 6,8,9), which modulate conjugate or horizontal eye movements. The inferior frontal gyrus is composed of pars opercularis, pars triangularis, and pars orbitalis. In the dominant hemisphere, Broca's area of speech (BA 44 and 45) is formed by the pars triangularis and pars opercularis. This region is responsible for the motor component of speech such as verbal fluency, grammar processing, attention, and phonological processing.

Occipital Lobe

The occipital lobe of the brain corresponds to the occipital bone of the skull. It is located in both the temporal and parietal lobes. This lobe is located superior to the tentorium cerebelli and the medial surface of the occipital lobe relates to the falx cerebri. The occipital lobe is separated from the parietal lobe and temporal lobe by the parietooccipital sulcus and lateral parietotemporal line, respectively. Three gyri are located on the superior and lateral surface of the occipital lobe—middle, inferior, and superior occipital gyri. The middle and superior occipital gyri are separated from each other via the intraoccipital sulcus, which is the continuation of the intraparietal sulcus. The lateral or inferior occipital sulcus separates the middle and superior occipital gyri from the inferior occipital gyrus. (Thau, 2021)

The medial surface of the occipital lobe is characterized by a fissure, termed the calcarine sulcus, which is posterior to the parietooccipital sulcus and superior to the occipital pole. The medial surface of the occipital is further divided into the cuneate gyrus superiorly and the lingual gyrus inferiorly by the calcarine sulcus. The calcarine sulcus is associated with the primary visual cortex (BA 17), which is related to visual perception. The rest of the occipital lobe is occupied by the visual association cortex or extrastriate visual cortex (BA 18 and 19) which is responsible for the interpretation of visual images. The occipital lobe is the visual processing center of the brain that is related to facial recognition, visuospatial processing, color determination, depth perception, and memory formation.

Temporal Lobe

The temporal lobe of the brain is located in the middle cranial fossa and is proximal to the temporal bone of the skull. The lateral sulcus anatomically separates the temporal lobe from the frontal and parietal lobes. The temporal lobe is associated with the auditory processing, memory, and sensory part of speech. The temporal lobe comprises the inferior, middle, and superior temporal gyri, predominantly on the lateral surface of the temporal lobe. These three gyri are anatomically separated by superior and inferior temporal sulci. The hippocampus comprises the inferiomedial region of the temporal lobe. (Thau, 2021)

The superior aspect of the superior temporal gyrus contains the primary auditory area (BA 41) or transverse gyri of Heschl. The primary auditory area is associated with the reception of auditory signals. The secondary auditory area (BA 42) is located in the superior temporal gyrus, behind the primary auditory area. This area receives information from the thalamus and primary auditory area. The function of visual perception is attributed to the inferior and middle temporal gyri. The middle temporal gyrus is responsible for movement perception in the visual field, whereas the inferior temporal gyrus comprises the fusiform face area, which is responsible for face recognition.

Insular Lobe

The fifth lobe of the brain, the insular lobe, is located deep in the lateral sulcus or Sylvian fissure. The insular lobe is visible upon retraction of the temporal lobe. Opercula are referred to as regions of parietal, temporal, and frontal lobes which surround the insular lobe.

The insular lobe is further divided into anterior and posterior regions by the central sulcus of the insula. The anterior region of the insular lobe is characterized by three gyri - posterior, anterior, and middle short gyri, in addition to an accessory gyrus. The posterior region of the insular lobe comprises anterior and posterior long gyri. The insular lobe of the brain is responsible for the integration and processing of taste, visceral, vestibular, and pain sensations.

Cerebrum and Cerebral Cortex

Prior sections have described the various components of the cerebrum or forebrain. This section will describe the anatomical and physiological features of the grey matter of the cerebrum, known as the cerebral cortex. The cerebral cortex is located just underneath the cranial pia matter.

The cerebral cortex comprises cell bodies of the neurons and is composed of folds and grooves called gyri and sulci respectively. This increases the surface area of the cerebral cortex, making it capable of greater cognition and learning abilities. The cerebral cortex is functionally subdivided into sensory, association, and motor areas. The cerebral cortex is associated with sensory awareness and perception, initiation and planning of motor movements, motivation, decision-making, attention, memory, learning, conceptual thinking, and problem-solving functions

Sulci present on the lateral surface of the cerebral hemisphere include lateral sulcus or Sylvian fissure and central sulcus. The medial surface of each cerebral hemisphere is characterized by the parietooccipital sulcus, cingulate sulcus, collateral sulcus, and circular sulcus of the insula. The layers of the cerebral cortex are denoted by Roman numerals. These layers, from superficial to deep, are listed as follows.

Molecular plexiform layer (I)

External granular layer (II)

External pyramidal layer (III)

Internal granular layer (IV)

Internal pyramidal layer (V)

Multiform fusiform layer (VI)

The cerebral cortex is functionally divided into primary, secondary, and associative regions. The primary areas of the cerebral cortex are responsible for the elementary motor and sensory functions. Secondary regions are located proximal to the primary areas. These areas receive afferent signals from the thalamus and other primary areas of the cerebral cortex. The secondary areas integrate signals received from the primary areas and thalamus to further refine the stimuli of the primary areas. Association areas of the cerebral cortex are responsible for the integration, processing, and analysis of different types of information and modulate the higher mental functions.

Cerebellum [d]

Cerebellum originates from the hindbrain or rhomboncephalon and is located in the posterior cranial fossa beneath the tentorium cerebelli. The cerebellum comprises an outer grey matter forming the cerebellar cortex and an inner white matter. It is associated superiorly with the great cerebral vein of Galen and the lingual gyrus of the occipital lobe of the cerebrum. The anterior relations of the cerebellum include the brainstem, medullary vela of the fourth ventricle, distal aspect of the cerebral aqueduct of Sylvius, corpora quadrigemini, foramen of Magendie, foramen magnum, medulla oblongata, and posterior cerebromedullary cistern. Similar to the cerebrum, cerebrospinal fluid (CSF) is also associated with the cerebellum. The posterior and lateral relations of the cerebellum include occipital bone and related dura matter, occipital sinus, the confluence of sinuses, and sigmoid sinuses. The cerebellum has superior or tentorial and inferior or occipital surfaces characterized by superior vermis and inferior vermis respectively. (Thau, 2021)

Brainstem

The brainstem is the distal portion of the brain which comprises pons, medulla oblongata, and the midbrain. Collectively, the brainstem is responsible for regulating blood pressure, breathing, and heart rate. The brainstem comprises the cranial nerve nuclei and important afferent and efferent pathways. The brainstem connects the brain tissue with the rest of the body. The brainstem extends anteriorly from the cerebral peduncles to the quadrigeminal plate posteriorly. The brainstem terminates as the medullary pyramids decussate at the level of the foramen magnum. The brainstem is divided vertically into the midbrain, pons, and medulla oblongata; and horizontally into the tectum and tegmentum at the level of the midbrain.

Limbic System

The limbic lobe of the brain encompasses the corpus callous, located on the medial surface of each cerebral hemisphere. The limbic lobe surrounds the ventricles of the brain and is located deep in the temporal, frontal, and parietal lobes. The limbic lobe is associated with visceral functions, autonomic functions, emotions, learning, memory, and hormonal functions.

White Matter and Grey Matter

As a general rule of thumb, white matter comprises the neuronal cell processes, whereas grey matter is simply a collection of neuronal cell bodies. In the brain, the grey matter lies exterior to the white matter. However, in the white matter, this arrangement is reversed. The outer layer of the grey matter is referred to as the cortex, forming the cerebellar cortex and cerebral cortex. The collection of grey matter in the inner aspect of the brain is known as the nucleus.

White matter is made of myelinated nerve fibers, hence the white color, and facilitates communication between different regions of the central nervous system. Common terms associated with white matter include tract, fasciculus, funiculus, stria, fibers, commissures, and decussation.

Important Pathways

Tracts are described as neural pathways which facilitate communication between the brain and the spinal cord. However, the tracts may be located entirely in the brain. Tracts are grossly divided into ascending and descending tracts which run from the spinal cord to the brain and brain to the spinal cord respectively. The CNS also comprises intracerebral tracts including basal ganglia and limbic system. The tracts are named according to the origin and termination of the neural pathways. The ascending tracts of the spinal cord are located as follows.

Gracile tract

Cuneate tract

Anterior spinothalamic tract

Lateral spinothalamic tract

Spinotectal tract

Spino-olivary tract

Anterior spinocerebellar tract

Posterior spinocerebellar tract

Spinoreticular tract

The descending tracts are listed as follows.

Lateral corticospinal tract

Anterior corticospinal tract

Corticobulbar tract

Rubrospinal tract

Reticulospinal tract

Lateral vestibulospinal tract

Medial vestibulospinal tract

Meninges

The bony structures, skull and vertebral column, and membranous structures, Meninges, warrant protection to the brain and spinal cord. Meninges are three membranous layers that ensheath the brain and spinal cord, as well as separate these structures from the skull and vertebral column. Cranial meninges surround the brain, whereas spinal meninges surround the spinal cord. Meninges include dura matter, arachnoid matter, and pia matter. The last two layers are collectively referred to as leptomeninges. Potential spaces related to the meninges include subarachnoid space, epidural space, and subdural space. The cerebrospinal fluid (CSF) runs between the arachnoid and pia matter in the subarachnoid space. (Herbet & Duffau, 2020)

Cranial Nerves

Cranial nerves are a set of 12 pairs of peripheral nerves that control a myriad of body functions. These nerves emerge from the brain and innervation structures in the head, neck, abdomen, and thorax. These nerves are responsible for carrying motor and/or sensory signals between the brain and the body. Afferent fibers carry sensory information from the periphery to the brain, whereas efferent fibers carry motor information from the brain to the periphery. Mixed nerves carry both motor and sensory information. The nerve fibers are further classified as general, special, visceral, and somatic.

Olfactory nerve (CN I)

The olfactory nerve is responsible for the perception of smell.

Optic nerve (CN II)

The optic nerve is responsible for the perception of vision.

Oculomotor nerve (CN III)

It innervates sphincter papillae, ciliary muscle, and extraocular muscles except for the superior oblique and lateral rectus.

Trochlear nerve (CN IV)

It innervates the superior oblique muscle.

Trigeminal nerve (CN V)

The trigeminal nerve provides sensory innervation to the face.

Abducens nerve (CN VI)

The abducens nerve is responsible for the innervation of the lateral rectus muscle of the eyeball.

Facial nerve (CN VII)

The facial nerve controls the facial expression, taste sensation, and secretory activity of the glands including submandibular, sublingual, palatine, basal, and lacrimal glands.

Vestibulocochlear nerve (CN VIII)

The cochlear nerve is responsible for hearing and the vestibular nerve is responsible for balance, posture, and motion. The two nerves converge in the internal acoustic meatus, giving rise to the vestibulocochlear nerve.

Glossopharyngeal nerve (CN IX)

Functions of the CN IX include swallowing, taste sensation, visceral and general sensation of the oral cavity, and salivation.

Vagus nerve (CN X)

The vagus nerve provides motor and sensory innervation to the structures present in the head, neck, abdomen, and thorax.

Accessory nerve (CN XI)

Functions of the glossopharyngeal nerve include head movements, shoulder movements, and phonation.

Hypoglossal nerve (CN XII)

The hypoglossal nerve innervates the muscles responsible for tongue movements and plays an integral role in speech and swallowing.

Ventricles and CSF

The ventricular system of the brain is responsible for the production and flow of CSF, which in turn provides protection to the brain. The ventricular system comprises lateral, third, and fourth ventricles. The structure that synthesizes the CSF is known as the choroid plexus. The choroid plexus is composed of tela choroidea (a vascular component of the pia matter), ependyma, and choroid epithelium. The CSF contains water, amino acids, glucose, and other plasma components essential for the nourishment and metabolic activity of the brain tissue. After traveling through the ventricular system, the CSF is absorbed into the subarachnoid space, where it functions as a shock absorbent. (Ackerman, 2022)

What is the brain made of?

Overview of Brain Histology

The CNS comprises neurons, microglia, and macroglia. Approximately 100 billion neurons are present in the brain, with a greater percentage of neuroglial cells as compared to neurons. Based on the origin, cells of the CNS are divided into two categories. Astrocytes, oligodendrocytes, neurons, and ependymocytes are the cells of neuroectodermal origin. On the contrary, blood vessels, meninges, adipose tissue, and microglia are the cells of mesenchymal origin.

Neurons

Types of Neurons

The neurons have a large cell body, also called perikaryon with a pale nucleus and prominent nucleolus. The cell processes include axons and dendrites. The neurons also contain Nissl bodies that are a collection of the rough endoplasmic reticulum. The size and shape of the neurons vary in different regions of the brain and spinal cord, and the neurons may be myelinated or unmyelinated. Oligodendrocytes myelinate the axons in the CNS, whereas Schwann cells myelinate the axons in the peripheral nervous system.

Neurons communicate with one another by neurotransmitters, which are small molecules released in response to a stimulus. A specialized area between the two neurons which is responsible for the transmission of nerve impulses or action potentials is called a synapse.

Neurons are classified based on a number of neuronal processes (axons and dendrites). The neurons can be unipolar, pseudounipolar, bipolar, and multipolar.

Multipolar neurons are located in the brain and spinal cord. Motor neurons and interneurons are classified as multipolar neurons. The cell body may be polygonal or fusiform, with one axon and several dendrites arising from the cell body.

Bipolar neurons are responsible for carrying the afferent impulses. These neurons are characterized by a single axon and single dendritic tree emerging from either end of an oval cell body. Bipolar neurons are present in the ocular, vestibulocochlear, and olfactory systems.

The unipolar neurons are characterized by a single axon protruding from a spherical cell body. However, these cells do not have dendritic branches. Unipolar neurons are present in the sensory ganglia and peripheral nerves.

The pseudounipolar neurons are characterized by a single neuronal process emerging from the cell body. This neuronal process bifurcates and forms an axon and a dendrite. Pseudounipolar cells are associated with joint position and proprioception. (Enache AL;Slujitoru AS;Pintea IL;Stocheci CM;Mateescu GO;Gheorghişor I, 2012)

Location of Neurons

This section discusses the composition and location of the neurons in the cortical layers of the cerebrum and cerebellum. The layers of the cerebral neocortex are described below.

Molecular layer (I) is the outermost layer that comprises terminal branches of the axons and dendrites. Axons originate from the thalamus and cerebral hemispheres, whereas dendrites emerge from the pyramidal cells. Retzius-Canal cells are present between the dendrites and axons.

The external granular layer (II) is composed of small pyramidal cells and interneurons.

The external pyramidal layer (III) comprises pyramidal cells. These cells are associated with the association and commissural fibers in the cerebral cortex.

The internal granular layer (IV) comprises pyramidal cells, interneurons, and stellate cells.

The internal pyramidal layer (V) is composed of large pyramidal cells of Betz. These cells are present in the primary motor cortex and responsible for sending signals to the spinal cord, subcortical areas, and brainstem.

The multiform layer (VI) comprises interneurons and pyramidal cells, with a greater majority of fusiform cells. Efferent fibers from this layer project to the claustrum and thalamus.

The cerebellar cortex is composed of the outer molecular layer, middle Purkinje cell layer, and inner granular layer. The molecular layer comprises a few small neurons, the middle layer comprises pyramidal cells, the dendritic branches of which project into the outer molecular layer. The inner layer has a greater quantity of small neurons.

Glial Cells

Glial cells or neuroglia are non-neuronal cells present in the CNS. Glial cells are responsible for the myelination, support, protection, and homeostatic balance of the neurons. Though smaller, these cells are more abundant than the neurons and have distinct morphologic and physiologic characteristics. Glial cells of the CNS include oligodendrocytes, microglia, ependymal cells, and astrocytes.

Oligodendrocytes

Oligodendrocytes are characterized by long cytoplasmic projections arising from the cell body, which is enriched with polyribosome and rough endoplasmic reticulum. These cells are more abundant in white matter. Oligodendrocytes are further divided into satellite oligodendrocytes which are adjacent to the cell bodies and interfascicular oligodendrocytes which are present between myelinated axons. These cells synthesize myelin, which facilitates saltatory conduction of nerve impulses. Myelin sheath diameter is proportional to the conduction velocity.

Microglia

Microglia comprise 5% of the total population of glial cells. These cells are characterized by elongated nuclei and sparse cytoplasm. Microglia are derived from the monocytes and are present in both the white and grey matter of the CNS. These cells are dormant in healthy individuals and function as immune effector cells in a disease state.

Ependymal cells

The ependymal cells are columnar or low cuboidal epithelial cells that line the ventricular system of the brain. The ependymal cells are categorized into tanycytes, choroidal epithelial cells, and ependymocytes. Choroidal epithelial cells have microvilli on the apical side and invaginations on the basal side. These cells are responsible for the regulation of the chemical composition of CSF. The ependymocytes are the most abundant of ependymal cells. These cells also have apical microvilli, however, the basal surfaces of these cells are marked by cytoplasmic extensions, which come in contact with the astrocytes. These cells facilitate communication between the neuronal tissue and CSF. The tanycytes have long basal processes which terminate at the pia matter. These cells are predominantly associated with the hypothalamus and floor of the third ventricle.

Astrocytes

Astrocytes are star-shaped glial cells with end feet. These cells contain cytoplasmic glial fibrillary acidic protein (GFAP). However, these proteins are very few in the adult gray matter and fetal brain. The end feet form glia limitans, associated with the pia matter. Astrocytes separate neuronal tissue from non-neuronal tissue. Astrocytes are classified into fibrous and protoplasmic astrocytes. The latter is present in the grey matter and is responsible for terminating the action potentials. Fibrous astrocytes are present in the white matter and have greater amounts of GFAP in the cytoplasm. The astrocytes maintain the ionic balance, support the neuronal tissue structurally and metabolically, and secrete growth factors that mediate the growth of the neuronal tissue. (Dayan, 1970)

Neural Stem Cells

The neural stem cells (NSCs) play a pivotal role in the development of the CNS. During the development, these cells line the neural tube and undergo both symmetric and asymmetric divisions. The three cell lines principally associated with the NSCs include neurons, astrocytes, and oligodendrocytes. Following the development of CNS and its further growth into an adult CNS, the NSCs tend to reduce in number and become restricted to certain regions of the brain. Experimental evidence is available for neurogenesis in the lateral ventricles, dentate gyrus, and hippocampus. The evidence demonstrates the potential for the utilization of these NSCs in the repair of neurons that are severed in an injury or disease. In adult rodents, NSCs are associated with olfactory function and learning. Adult neurogenesis is modulated by diseases such as stroke, depression, injury, and epilepsy. One shall note that aging influences the process of adult neurogenesis negatively. Age-associated alterations in the peripheral immune cells and blood-borne factors are responsible for the reduced efficiency of adult neurogenesis as a person ages.

Blood Vessels in the Brain

Arterial Supply of Brain

The brain is a highly perfumed organ, owing to its extensive metabolic activity and role in controlling and regulating body functions. Pairs of internal carotid arteries and vertebral arteries supply oxygenated blood to the tissues of the brain. The internal carotid arteries are responsible for supplying blood to the cerebrum while the vertebral arteries coalesce to form the basilar artery, branches of these two arteries supply oxygenated blood to the brainstem and cerebellum. The basilar artery further joins the internal carotid artery as well as communicating arteries to form a structure known as the circle of Willis. This structure is the origin of anterior, posterior, and middle cerebral arteries, which gives rise to further arteries and arterioles that supply blood to different aspects of the cerebral cortex.

Pial arteries are important entities in the CNS and present on the brain surface in the glia limitans. These vessels are surrounded by the CSF and give rise to penetrating arterioles that are present in the Virchow-Robin space, which is an extension of the subarachnoid space. As these vessels penetrate the brain tissue, they become parenchyma arterioles and are surrounded by the end feet processes of astrocytes.

Venous Drainage of Brain

The venous system of the brain comprises cerebral veins and dural venous sinuses, which are interconnected and communicate freely. The cerebral venous outflow is made of valveless veins that are deep or central veins and superficial cortical veins. The superficial cortical veins lie on the cerebral surface in the pia matter. These veins drain blood from the subcortical white matter and cerebral cortex. The central veins comprise subependymal veins, great vein of Galen, and basal vein. These veins drain blood from the deeper regions of grey and white matter associated with the basal cistern, lateral ventricle, and third ventricle. These veins join the cortical veins and drain the blood into the superior sagittal sinus. The blood then flows through the confluence of sinuses, sigmoid sinuses, and jugular veins. The occipital sinuses along with inferior cerebellar veins are responsible for the drainage of blood from the cerebellum. The venous drainage of the brainstem is associated with the transverse and inferior petrosal sinuses. While peripheral veins contain valves, the cerebral veins have a peculiar nature of being valveless. As compared to cerebral arteries, the cerebral veins are thin-walled. In contrast to veins in the cerebral parenchyma, the larger pial veins are characterized by circumferential smooth muscle.

The neurovascular unit of the brain is referred to as the capillary bed in the brain, which comprises intercommunicating vessels containing specialized endothelial cells and devoid of smooth muscle. Capillaries of the human brain are approximately 400 miles (643.74 kilometers) long and serve as a rich site for the exchange of nutrients and oxygen. It is even considered that each neuron of the brain has its capillary. The density of the capillary bed in the brain is determined by the location of the capillaries and the metabolic demand of that region. Environmental and pathological factors determine the changes in the density of the capillary bed. Chronic hypoxia of the neuronal tissues may activate the angiogenic pathways, which in turn increase the capillary density of the relevant region. (Jeans & Esiri, 2008)

Collateral circulation is responsible for maintaining the blood flow in the human brain. The collateral circulation provides an alternate route to the blood flow supply when the principal pathways become constricted or occluded. Present at the base of the brain, the circle of Willis is responsible for the redistribution of the circulation when the large intracranial or extracranial vessels become occluded. The circle of Willis mediates the low resistance flow of the blood and provides collateral support to the cerebral circulations.

The discovery of the electroencephalogram

Introduction to EEG

Electroencephalogram, abbreviated as EEG, is a useful tool for assessing the electrical activity of the brain. It is also pivotal to the evaluation of seizures and health conditions that are similar to seizures. It is also used for the assessment of comatose patients, encephalopathies, and the types of seizures. EEG recording involves the placement of electrodes over the scalp, followed by the measurement of the absolute electrical potentials, which are generated by the cerebral cortex neurons. The cerebral cortex area required for the deflection on the EEG of the scalp is estimated to be 10 cm^2. Pyramidal cell bodies, associated with the electrical activity of the brain on EEG, are present in the cerebral cortical layers 3 and 5. These cells generate excitatory and inhibitory postsynaptic potentials, determined by the decolonization or hyperpolarization of the neurons. The summation of excitatory and inhibitory postsynaptic potentials over a predetermined cortical region influences the positive or negative deflection, which is measured by the EEG. The dipoles are oriented parallel to the plane of pyramidal cells in the cerebral cortex.

Feedback linkages connect the subcortical structures with the cortical neurons. Sinusoidal rhythmic activity is recorded on the EEG when the person is in a relaxed or resting state. This rhythm is also known as posterior dominant rhythm, which arises as a result of the oscillatory relationship between the subcortical structures and the cerebral cortex. For instance, the relationship between the thalamus, a subcortical structure, and the visual cortex, a component of the cerebral cortex. In an activated state, the oscillatory activity on the EEG is replaced by activity with faster frequency and lower amplitude. In the background of seizures, the abnormal brain network gives rise to a large super-synchronous neuronal discharge. EEG evaluation of such events provides necessary information related to the spread and localization of these neuronal discharges. More prevalent frequencies associated with EEG include alpha, beta, theta, and delta with a frequency range of 8-12 Hz, 13-30 Hz, 4-7 Hz, and less than 4 Hz respectively. The occurrence of these waves is determined by the state of wakefulness or alertness of the individual, along with his or her age. EEG waveforms in the prenatal stage have a discontinuous background, whereas the EEG waveforms mature as a person grows older. The posterior dominant rhythm in adults is 8.5 Hz during the resting state. Slower waveforms predominantly occur during wakefulness and later stages of sleep. Moreover, waveforms with faster frequencies are located in the anterior region of the brain, whereas waveforms with slower frequencies are present in the posterior regions of the brain. (Biasiucci et al., 2019)

Pioneers of EEG

Richard Caton

Richard Caton, an English scientist, is considered a pioneer of EEG. He discovered the electrical properties of the brain in 1875. He used a galvanometer, a device to measure electric current, to observe the electrical impulses of the brain. Caton reported the findings of his experiment to the British Medical Association in 1875, to the British Medical Journal supplement in 1877, and the Ninth International Medical Congress, in Washington DC in 1887. In his experiment, he placed unipolar electrodes over the surface of two cerebral hemispheres or placed one electrode over the skull surface and the other on the gray matter or cerebral cortex. He used Thomson's galvanometer to measure the electric currents via optical magnification of e meniscus. He observed that the electric currents increase with sleep. The baseline variations in the electric currents were not associated with the respiratory and cardiac rhythms. These currents were aborted after the death of the experimental animal and were sensitive to anesthesia and anoxia of these animals. Caton also discovered a strong association between the variation of electric currents and exposure to light. (EK;Frey, 2016)

Fleischel von Marxow

Fleischel von Marxow also contributed to the development of the first EEG. He studied evoked potentials and linked the activity of the nervous system with muscle movements. (Biasiucci et al., 2019)

Dr. Hans Berger

Hans Berger is known for recording the first EEGs in humans in 1924. He initially aimed to assess and discover the psychological mechanisms underlying physical phenomena, however, he failed to obtain satisfactory results. He continued working on the investigation of the electrical activity of the human brain. He gave birth to the term, electroencephalogram, and identified the alpha and beta wave patterns. He published a paper relevant to his experiments in 1929. In his paper, he described a wide array of normal and abnormal activity of the human brain on EEG. These include changes in the electrical activity of the brain on EEG related to mental effort, attention, and cerebral injury. Berger also elaborated on the intellectual changes in the brain following prefrontal cortex injuries, in 1920. In 1923, he described the preservation of the tissue after frontal lobe damage.

Conclusion

EEG is pivotal to the assessment of the electrical activity of the brain. It is also associated with neurofeedback training, as described in the previous chapters. The pioneers of EEG who contributed significantly to its development include Richard Caton, Fleischel von Marxow, and Hans Berger. These individuals identify the electrical activity of the brain in both animal and human experiment models and developed the foundation for the application of EEG in diverse medical fields.

What is measured with the EEG?

Brief Overview of EEG

EEG is used for the detection, assessment, and evaluation of the electrical activity of the brain. It uses electrodes, unipolar or bipolar, which are placed over certain areas of the scalp, which correspond to specific areas of the cerebral cortex of the brain. The EEG is based on the fact that the neurons communicate with each other through electrical impulses, and the electrical activity of the brain varies in different physiological and pathological states. Not only does EEG evaluate the electrical activity of the brain in comatose patients, but it is also an important diagnostic tool in epilepsy and the onset of seizures. It is also used for the diagnosis of brain tumors, injury-associated damage to the brain tissue, sleep disorders, inflammation of the brain, stroke, and brain dysfunction. EEG is a useful tool for confirming death in comatose patients. Read the following sections to learn about the indications, prerequisites, and complications of EEG. (EK;Frey, 2016)

How Does EEG Measure Electrical Activity of the Brain?

Before jumping onto the measurement of the electrical activity of the brain, it is important to discuss the equipment required for performing EEG. EEG is performed by a trained and experienced EEG technician or technologist. A clinical neurophysiologist then reviews the EEG findings and generates a report. The basic equipment for EEG includes electrodes, an EEG system, and an amplifier. The electrodes commonly used for EEG are silver or silver-chloride electrodes. The EEG system includes a monitor and a processor. The current clinical practices use the standard EEG system, which is capable of acquiring information from a minimum of 128 channels with a sample rate of more than 10 kHz and a resolution of 24-bits in each amplifier. EEG assessment also requires the application of gels and salts over the scalp surface to improve the electrical conductivity of the scalp and the record waveforms. The process of scalp preparation is further enhanced by the introduction of dry electrodes, which do not require the application of gel over the scalp surface.

EEG assessment is usually conducted in a quiet room that also has controllable lighting levels. The scalp electrodes are placed according to the 10 to 20 international system. Typical EEG assessment requires 21 electrodes which are placed on the scalp of an adult. These electrodes also include ground and reference electrodes. After the placement of electrodes over the scalp, the EEG technician or technologist measures the electrode impedance and ensures that the impedance is below 5 kohms. Before initiating the EEG assessment, the calibration shall also be performed. Calibration involves biological calibration and recording or a square wave signal. Activation procedures are performed while recording the electrical activity of the brain to trigger EEG changes such as opening and closing of eyes, phonic stimulation, hyperventilation, and epileptiform abnormalities. Recordings of state of sleep and drowsiness are integral components of EEG assessment. Sleep deprivation is a provocative technique used in the EEG recording of the electrical activity of the brain. The difference in electrical potential between two electrodes of a single channel shows deflection on the EEG. The bipolar and referential montages are useful for accurate isolation and localization of the abnormal neuronal discharges in the brain. Commonly used montages in EEG include referential, laplacian, and bipolar montages.

Indications of EEG

The indications of EEG are listed as follows.

EEG facilitates the classification of the types of seizures an individual is suffering from. It is also useful for the localization of the onset of seizures.

The Wada test or sodium amobarbital test is useful for determining the cerebral hemisphere which is dominant for memory and language.

EEG is also useful for the induction of therapeutic coma and for managing individuals suffering from status epilepticus.

Individuals with an altered mental state, arising from toxic metabolic encephalopathies and other etiologies, tend to undergo EEG assessment of the electrical activity of the brain.

Individuals suffering from encephalopathies without specific etiologies undergo an EEG assessment of the electrical activity of the brain to identify the degree or severity of the encephalopathy.

Individuals presenting with syncope or symptoms associated with loss of consciousness accompanied by negative cardiac workup also undergo EEG assessment of the electrical activity of the brain.

Comatose patients with decreased responsiveness, persistent confusion, or impaired mental status, admitted to the intensive care units, are candidates for EEG assessment of the electrical activity of the brain.

Prognostication following sudden cardiac arrest also requires an EEG assessment of the electrical activity of the brain.

EEG is also performed for the identification of delayed ischemic changes associated with intracranial and subarachnoid hemorrhages.

EEG is associated with anesthetic procedures conducted for monitoring the depth of anesthesia.

EEG is an important tool for determining and declaring brain death, particularly in comatose patients.

Contradictions of EEG

The contraindications of EEG are not clearly defined or established.

Electrode placement is a challenging task in individuals who have undergone craniotomy as well as in individuals who have open wounds or breaches in the skull.

If seizures or epilepsy are suspected, an EEG shall be performed one detailed history of the patient be obtained.

People with specific underlying conditions shall not be subjected to activation procedures of EEG. Hyperventilation is considered a relative contraindication in individuals with a prior history of transplant surgeries, stroke, acute respiratory distress syndrome, myocardial infarction, sickle cell anemia, asthma, and Moyamoya disease. (EK;Frey, 2016)

Prerequisites of EEG

Following are the prerequisites and preparation measures for performing EEG.

The patients are recommended against the usage of conditioners before their EEG appointment, as these substances may cause electrode impedance and hinder the quality of recording of the electrical activity of the brain.

Before starting EEG assessment, the scalp of the patient is cleaned thoroughly to eliminate dirt and debris, which may cause electrode impedance.

The electrode impedance shall be less than 5 kilohm, for accurate and precise measurement of the electrical activity of the brain.

For patients who are admitted to the intensive care units, certain measures must be undertaken to reduce disturbances originating from medical instruments while keeping the electrode impedance minimal.

Medical restraints are required at certain times for obtaining a proper and accurate recording of the electrical activity of the brain on EEG.

Risks and Complications of EEG

The complications and risks of EEG are listed down below.

The complication associated with EEG may arise due to a lack of diligence during the screening of the patients before performing the provocative or activation procedures.

EEG monitoring of patients in intensive care units and epilepsy monitoring units over longer periods is associated with an increased risk for skin injury. Hence, appropriate care must be provided to such patients.

Conclusion

EEG is an important tool used for the assessment of the electrical activity of the brain. The indications for EEG include brain injury, epilepsy, and other seizure-associated abnormalities, diagnosis of encephalopathies, monitoring, and evaluation of comatose patients, prognostication following sudden cardiac arrest, identification of ischemic brain changes, and induction of therapeutic coma. EEG is performed by a trained EEG technologist and utilizes a set of equipment including an EEG system comprising a monitor and processor, an amplifier, and electrodes. Gels and salts are also applied to the scalp area while placing the electrodes, to enhance the conductivity of electrical signals of the brain. The EEG shall be performed according to the given set of guidelines in a quiet room. Hyperventilation is a relative contraindication in a certain group of patients.

Basics of learning theory

Introduction to Learning Theory

Learning refers to the change in behavior, which is a product of previous experiences. The learning theory explains the process by which individuals collect and accommodate, process, store, and retrieve the knowledge in the process of learning. In addition to prior experiences of an individual, the environmental, emotional, and cognitive processes also play an important role in the learning processes. Motivation drives the process of learning and is involved in the sustained learning processes of an individual. The widely accepted theories of learning include behaviorism theory, cognitivism theory, constructivism theory, sociocultural theory, and critical or humanism theory. (Badyal & Singh, 2017)

Behaviourism Theory

The behaviorism theory implies that learning is a change in behavior that occurs in the desired direction. The behavioral changes in the desired direction occur in response to the application of various techniques. These techniques include encouragement and rewards for promoting the correct behavior in an individual. The corrections in behavior are made and sustained by the repetition of correct behaviors, feedback of behavior, and reinforcement for demonstration of correct behavior. The behaviorism theory is based on the external stimulus and demonstration of associated behavior. The theory involves the skill and drill exercise and modulates correct behaviors by continuous repetition of the behaviors. (Gandhi & Mukherji, 2021)

Cognitivism Theory

Cognitivism theory is the second learning theory, and it is associated with the restructuring of internal cognition in response to the changes in an individual's knowledge. Based on this theory, the learners utilize cognitive tools such as perceptions, memory, information processing, and insight to facilitate learning and enhance cognitive performance. Cognitivism theory involves the acquisition, storage, and retrieval of information for optimal functioning. Learners gradually become capable of self-directed learning. Under this theory, individuals learn how to learn.

Constructivism Theory

The third learning theory, constructivism theory, describes how the newer understanding of an individual develops on the foundation of existing knowledge and understanding of that individual. The learners build the new knowledge because of their experiencess knowledge with their physical, mental, and biological stages of development. The learners collect and accommodate the new knowledge and apply this knowledge to acquire a newer understanding. Based on this theory, the learning processes involve the use of critical reflections to derive and construct meaning from knowledge and experiences.

Sociocultural Theory

The sociocultural theory considers the process of learning to be a social phenomenon, in which learning occurs in a sociocultural context. Based on this theory, the learner functions as a full member of the community or do so in the capacity of apprenticeship. Learning is related to both the environment and people. Medication education usually occurs in the setting of a workplace, where the sociocultural theory is applicable.

Critical Theory

The critical learning theory describes ways in which one can change society to make changes for all individuals. This is done by encouraging the learners to participate, particularly those learners who are subjected to oppression or marginalization. The critical or humanism theory describes the learning of an individual is associated with his or her growth, both as a human being and as a professional. The critical theory of learning is subjected to different challenges that include exploration of emotions and modifications of identity. The main goal of the critical theory of learning is for the learner to gain autonomy and self-direction. Self-directed learning is among the most significant principles of critical or humanism theory of learning.

Clinical Significance of Learning Theory

The learning theories discussed above can be applied to both academic and healthcare settings. In the healthcare context, learning theories can be utilized by healthcare professionals to educate their patients, improve their adherence to the treatment measures, and improve the prognosis and treatment outcomes.

Conclusion

Learning is associated with changes in the behavior of an individual, which are the result of experiences of that individual. The learning theory focuses on the ways in which a person acquires, processes, stores, and recalls the knowledge. The process of learning is associated with experiences, environmental, emotional, and cognitive factors. The learning theories include behaviorism theory, cognitivism theory, constructivism theory, sociocultural theory, and critical or humanism theory. These theories can be applied in the healthcare setting to enhance patient compliance, yield positive treatment outcomes, and promote the education of the patients.

Operant conditioning

Introduction to Operant Conditioning

Operant behaviors are behaviors that are controlled by their consequences. Operant conditioning is referred to the study of reversible behaviors, which are maintained by using reinforcement schedules. A reinforcement schedule can be described as a procedure, which delivers a reinforcer as per a specific rule. For hungry animals, the reinforcer is usually food, delivered upon pressing a level or closure of a switch. Different reinforcers can be used for the human subjects.

History of Operant Conditioning

History of the operant conditioning and behaviors dates back to the twentieth century. John B. Watson is known as the founder of behaviorism. The first person to describe operant conditioning is B. F. Skinner. He developed experimental methods comprising learning animals and treated them as physiological preparations. He described reflexive behavior, which is associated with a stimulus, and operant behavior, which is not associated with a prior stimulus. (Station & Cerutti, 2003)

Components and Principles of Operant Conditioning

The principal components of operant conditioning are known as reinforcement and punishment. Both these components can be negative or positive. Positive reinforcement strengthens a specific behavior, whereas negative reinforcement eliminates a specific undesirable behavior. Similarly, positive punishment comprises the demonstration of an unfavorable event that will decrease the likelihood of response, whereas negative punishment refers to the elimination of a favorable event after a certain behavior is repeated. Responses of operant conditioning are further classified into neutral operants, punishers, and reinforcers. The neutral operants refer to those responses which do not modify the occurrence of certain behavior. Reinforcers refer to responses that increase the likelihood of repetition of certain behaviors. Lastly, punishers are those responses that reduce the likelihood of repetition of certain behaviors. The principles of operant conditioning include the following.

The positively reinforced behaviors will be repeated.

For the reinforcement of responses, the information must be provided in small bits.

The reinforcements are generalized for similar stimuli and produce secondary conditioning.

Applications of Operant Conditioning

Operant conditioning techniques can be applied to produce behavioral modifications in the targeted individuals. Individuals suffering from obesity, alcoholism, delinquency, aggression, and smoking benefit from operant conditioning techniques. Individuals suffering from anorexia nervosa, an eating disorder, become healthy and gain weight after being subjected to operant conditioning and associated behavioral modifications. The token economy method is part of operant conditioning and is useful for increasing the frequency of desired behaviors in the targeted individuals. The principles and techniques of operant conditioning have been implemented in mental and academic institutions successfully. (Staddon & Cerutti, 2003)

Transfer to everyday life: classical conditioning

Introduction to Classical Conditioning

Classical conditioning can be defined as an unconscious learning method. It is the simplest way to define the learning processes in human beings. In classical conditioning, a combination of specific stimuli and automatic conditioned responses is applied. The most thorough and descriptive work regarding classical conditioning has been done by Ivan Pavlov, who was a Russian physiologist. His study related to classical conditioning is commonly regarded as Pavlovian conditioning.

Pavlov's Experiment—The Origin of Classical Conditioning

The discovery of classical conditioning was accidental. While Pavlov was conducting an experiment related to digestion in dogs, he observed that the reactions of the dogs to the food tend to change over time. Initially, the dogs only salivated upon placement of food in front of them. In the later stages, the dogs salivated only slightly upon placement of food in front of them. He realized that the dogs salivated in response to the noises before the arrival of food, such as when the food cart is approaching the site where the dogs are located. Pavlov tested his theory by setting up an experiment. In this experiment, he rang a bell a short time before the food was presented to the dogs. Initially, the dogs did not salivate, however, in the later stages, the dogs began to salivate in response to the ringing of the bell regardless of the arrival of the food. (Rehman, 2021)

Contingency

The contingency theory of classical conditioning is assuming that there exists a contingent relationship between unconditioned and conditioned stimuli, which determine classical conditioning. Evidence demonstrates that contingency between conditioned and unconditioned stimuli is not necessarily required for classical conditioning.

Latent Inhibition

Latent inhibition in classical conditioning is described as the process by which the learning of the associations is inhibited these associations are first presented with the neural stimulus, therefore, representing non-association. This is characterized by the ability of novel and non-reinforced stimuli to suppress learning related to response to the stimulus. Latent inhibition is a non-contingent demonstration of how a stimulus suppresses the ability to affiliate with associations. This is also called learned irrelevance or learned inattention.

Overshadowing

In classical conditioning, overshadowing is referred to as the shadowing of a weaker stimulus by a stronger stimulus. This leads to a decline in classical conditioning with a weaker stimulus as compared to a stronger one. Hence, overshadowing is characterized by the weakening of the association of another stimulus in the presence of a stronger stimulus. (Rehman, 2021)

Blocking

In addition to other phenomena, blocking has been described in the studies associated with Pavlovian conditioning. Repeated exposure of the dog to a specific tone, which is the first conditioned stimulus, with the food, which is an unconditioned stimulus, leads to salivation in when upon exposure to the tone, this is termed a conditioned response. Further experimentation with two conditioned stimuli, tone and light, lead to a lack of salivation response upon exposure to light alone. The initial pairing of tone with the food has blocked the stimulus control with the second conditioned stimulus, the light.

Clinical Significance of Classical Conditioning

Classical conditioning is a form of learning, just like operant conditioning. The Pavlovian principles are known to influence the health, motivation, treatment of psychological disorders, and emotions of human beings. Drug counselors utilize the principles of classical conditioning to facilitate people in overcoming drug addictions. Classical conditioning is also known to influence the immune system of humans. Classical conditioning has also helped people in overcoming their phobias. Reconditioning of behaviors is an important measure for individuals, particularly children, with complaints of bed-wetting. Counterconditioning is an important technique for the effective management of phobias. Exposure and aversive therapies are the two counterconditioning techniques that help people overcome their phobias. (Rehman et al., 2021)

Can all brain structures be influenced by neurofeedback?

Overview of Functional Areas of Brain

The functional areas of the brain include the sensory, motor, and association areas. The motor cortex of the brain is associated with the planning, execution, and control of the voluntary motor movement of the body. The primary motor cortex is responsible for the initiation of motor movements whereas the non-primary motor cortical areas, including supplementary motor and premotor areas, are associated with the planning, initiation, and precision of the body movements. The cerebral hemispheres control the movements of the opposite half of the body. The motor cortex is predominantly located in the frontal lobe of the brain. The sensory cortical areas of the brain include the primary visual cortex of the occipital lobe, the primary auditory cortex of the temporal lobe, and the primary somatosensory cortex of the parietal lobe of the brain. Association areas of the cerebral cortex are responsible for the processing of motor and sensory information from the sensory and motor cortices of the brain. These areas are responsible for higher-order functions that include memory, speech, and learning.

Neurofeedback Training and Frontal Lobe

The neurofeedback training of the frontal lobe of the brain involves the placement of electrodes over FP_1, FP_2, F_3, F_4, F_7, FZ, and FPZ regions of the scalp and corresponding brain regions. Neurofeedback training of the frontal lobe is important for time management, emotions, empathy, character, and both short-term and long-term attention.

Neurofeedback Training and Parietal Lobe

In neurofeedback training of the parietal lobe of the brain, the electrodes are placed over P_3, P_4, and PZ. This neurofeedback training is associated with the naming of objects, solving problems, mathematical processing, construction of sentences, map orientation, space recognition, and complex grammar. The right and left parietal lobes of the brain are associated with distinct functions.

Neurofeedback Training and Temporal Lobe

During neurofeedback training of the temporal lobe of the brain, the electrodes are placed over T_3, T_4, T_5, and T_6. Functions of the left temporal lobe include word recognition while reading, learning, positive mood, and memory. In contrast to this, the right hemisphere temporal lobe is associated with anxiety, facial recognition, music, and understanding of direction.

Neurofeedback Training and Occipital Lobe

Neurofeedback training of the occipital lobe of the brain involves the placement of electrodes O_2, O_1, and O_z. Neurofeedback training of this lobe is associated with traumatic memories, accurate reading, visual memories, and visual flashbacks. The occipital lobe also facilitates the localization of objects in surroundings, spelling, reading, writing, and identification of colors and drawings.

Neurofeedback Training and Basal Ganglia-Thalamo-Cortical Loops

The basal ganglia-thalamo-cortical loops are associated with flexibility in the behaviors. The decline in the dopamine levels in the basal ganglia is associated with Parkinson's disease. The thalamus relays the information from the periphery to the cerebral cortex of the brain. The thalamic pathways are regulated by the activity of the reticular nucleus. Neurofeedback training of the basal ganglia-thalamo-cortical loops modulates the optimal function of the loop.

Neurofeedback Training and Cingulate Cortex

Neurofeedback training of the cingulate gyrus involves the placement of electrodes over O_z, F_z, FP_z, C_z, P_z, and O_z. Neurofeedback training attention, mental flexibility, cooperation, morals, and motivation. Abnormalities of the cingulate gyrus manifest as compulsions, tics, obsessions, ASD, obsessive-compulsive disorder (OCD), and perfectionism.

Which clinical pictures can be treated with neurofeedback?

Neurofeedback for Stroke Rehabilitation

Stroke is a neurological condition characterized by the abnormal electrical activity of the brain and the impairment of cognitive, sensory, and motor functions of the brain. Neurofeedback training is a cost-effective and non-invasive technique to induce neuroplasticity, promote positive behavior performance, and contribute to the stroke rehabilitation in the affected individuals. Neurofeedback training for stroke rehabilitation enhances the activity of the alpha waves in the brain and improves the cognitive functions of the training recipients. Alpha neurofeedback training also alleviates depression and anxiety in these patients. (Nan et al., 2019)

Neurofeedback for Learning Disabilities

Neurofeedback training is an effective approach for the treatment and management of learning disabilities such as dyscalculia and dyslexia. Dyslexia patients have difficulties in spelling and reading, whereas individuals with dyscalculia face challenges related to math problems. Neurofeedback treats learning disabilities by increasing the activity of alpha waves in the brain.

Neurofeedback for Addiction

Neurofeedback training plays an integral role in the resolution of drug addiction while reducing the craving and temptation of drugs. Neurofeedback training is an effective therapeutic measure for alcoholism, computer games addiction, and cocaine addiction. (Nan et al., 2019)

Neurofeedback for ADHD

ADHD is characterized by the malfunctioning of the frontal lobe of the brain. The symptoms of this disorder include distractibility, hyperactivity, and inattention. Medications for ADHD are not clinically effective and are associated with adverse effects such as decreased appetite, abdominal pain, headache, insomnia, anxiety, and irritability. When compared to healthy subjects, individuals with ADHD tend to have slower activity of beta and theta brain waves. The aim of neurofeedback training is to restore the normal behaviors in ADHD patients, without relying on pharmacological formulations or behavioral therapy. Neurofeedback training lowers the theta brain activity and increases beta activity in the brain. In other words, neurofeedback training aims to decrease the theta/beta ratio at the electrode. Neurofeedback training reduces hyperactivity and improves focus and sustained attention in ADHD patients.

Neurofeedback for Depression

Depression can be described by hypometabolism in different regions of the brain including the cingulate, insula, anterior temporal cortices, frontal cortex, thalamus, amygdala, and basal ganglia. Patients suffering from depression without significant anxiety demonstrate decreased activation of the right parietal lobe. Neurofeedback training alleviates depression by suppressing faster beta waves while increasing the activity of the alpha and theta waves.

Neurofeedback for Anxiety

Anxiety can be described as an increase in muscle tension. Since anxiety is associated with the inhibition of alpha waves, alpha wave neurofeedback training may alleviate anxiety. Furthermore, electromyogram (EMG) biofeedback for both specific and generalized patterns of anxiety.

Neurofeedback for Autism

ASD is referred to as a neurodevelopmental disorder, the symptoms, and challenges of which persist through adulthood. Children diagnosed with ASD face difficulties in verbal communication, non-verbal communication, interests, behavior, and social interaction. ASD is also associated with mental retardation, seizure disorders, and emotional problems. Autistic children develop extreme sensitivity to smells and sound as well as demonstrate poor social interaction, obsessive rumination, and idiosyncratic behavior. The diagnostic characteristics of ASD include high beta activity associated with anxiety; high delta/theta activity associated with impulsivity, hyperactivity, and lack of attention; and seizure activity. Approximately 50-60% of ASD patients demonstrate high beta activity. Neurofeedback training for ASD patients enhances the beta wave activity and inhibits the theta/alpha ratio.

Neurofeedback for PTSD

Neurofeedback is an alternative therapeutic approach for individuals who are suffering from post-traumatic stress disorder (PTSD). It is a debilitating health condition that arises after a life-threatening traumatic event. The symptoms of PTSD include avoidance of stimuli associated with the trauma, reexperiencing the event, changes in the cognition and mood, and hyperarousal of the affected individual. Exposure therapy is effective for the treatment of PTSD. However, it is an excruciating experience for the patient. The neurofeedback training sessions involve the induction of PTSD-associated activity of the brain. The frequency of the electrical activity can be altered after the feedback sessions. A novel neurofeedback training procedure, Decoded Neurofeedback (DecNef), is integrated into the clinical therapeutic approaches for the treatment of PTSD. This form of neurofeedback has greater advantages over conventional neurofeedback training, such that DecNef regulates the representation of certain stimuli in the brain, enables the training recipients to stimulate ideal patterns of brain activation, and infer the cause of the pattern of brain activity in PTSD patients.

Neurofeedback for Epilepsy

Medications formulated for the treatment of epilepsy are clinically ineffective in a significant percentage of individuals suffering from epilepsy. Effective treatment for such patients is neurofeedback training. Reduced slow rhythms with a frequency range of 4-7 Hz and increased SMR with a frequency range of 12-15 Hz are diagnostic characteristics of epilepsy. Continuous SMR treatment in epilepsy patients modulates uncontrolled epilepsy and lowers the rate of seizures.

Neurofeedback for Sleep Disorders

Insomnia is an epidemic sleeping disorder. Insomnia patients derive greater benefits from neurofeedback training as it improves sleep patterns of insomnia patients and improves the quality of sleep. With neurofeedback training, individuals are able to sleep faster. Neurofeedback training is performed for 30 minutes at 15-18 Hz frequency, using a single electrode. This method of neurofeedback training assists the therapy recipients in waking up faster. In contrast to this, the calmness treatment is performed at a frequency range of 12-15 Hz.

Neurofeedback for Neurodegenerative Disorders

Neurodegenerative disorders including dementia are referred to as gradual loss of the behavioral and cognitive functions in the affected individuals. These disorders are characterized by neuronal damage and subsequent death of the neurons. Individuals suffering from neurodegenerative disorders are vulnerable to difficulties in routine life activities. The risk and onset of neurodegenerative disorder increase as a person grow older. The current treatment strategies largely focus on reducing the rate at which cognitive function is deteriorating and alleviating the symptoms of these disorders. Neurofeedback training is considered a potential complementary therapeutic approach for the treatment and management of neurodegenerative disorders. Neurofeedback training uses a combination of cognitive training and operant conditioning. (Kober et al., 2017)

Neurofeedback for Borderline Personality Disorder

Neurofeedback-aided down regulation of the amygdala is an integral therapeutic approach for the treatment and management of borderline personality disorder (BPD). Neurofeedback training for BPD involved real-time fMRI, which directly targets the underlying neurobiological mechanisms of BPD. BPD is primarily characterized by emotional dysregulation including increased reactivity to negative environmental stimuli and impairment in the application of emotion regulation strategies as well as increased or exaggerated responses to the negative effects. In individuals with BPD, the amygdala demonstrates hyperactivity, culminating in emotional dysregulation. fMRI neurofeedback training, in addition to booster sessions, promote stable emotional regulation effects in BPD patients.

Neurofeedback for Speech and Language Impairment

Speech and language impairments hinder the communication between individuals. Speech and language impairments not only deteriorate the quality of life and overall health of the affected individuals, but also influence the professional proceedings of an individual's life. The assessment and treatment of speech and language impairments can be performed by evaluating the EEG measurements of the brain electrical activity as the affected individuals perform cognitive exercises during the treatment. These EEG evaluations also involve the comparison between the EEG findings in affected individuals vs. EEG findings in normal, healthy individuals without speech and language impairments. Speech or Linguistic Neurofeedback training targets certain regions of the brain to provide rehabilitation to the affected individuals.

Neurofeedback for Fibromyalgia

Fibromyalgia is characterized by widespread chronic pain, which is related to cognitive impairments as well as sleep disturbances. Fibromyalgia deteriorates the overall health of an individual and the quality of the life. This chronic pain condition is associated with increased activity and sensitivity of the brain areas concerned with the reception of pain, accompanied by decreased activity of the brain regions responsible for the inhibition of pain signals. Neurofeedback training for individuals suffering from fibromyalgia improves the perception of pain in these individuals and enhances the ability of the brain for the autoregulation of pain perception. Neurofeedback training also alleviates depression and anxiety, which are otherwise common in fibromyalgia patients.

Conclusion

Neurofeedback training is a cost-effective, non-invasive, and safe (when performed diligently and according to the given guidelines by a trained and experienced EEG technician or technologist) therapeutic approach for the treatment of a variety of health disorders. Neurofeedback training has proven to be effective for stroke rehabilitation, learning disabilities, addiction disorders, ADHD, ASD, depression, anxiety, panic attacks, PTSD, epilepsy, sleep disorders, neurodegenerative disorders, borderline personality disorder, fibromyalgia, and speech and language impairments.

Frequency band training

Introduction to Frequency Band Training

Frequency band training or classic neurofeedback training involves the use of certain frequencies that are trained during EEG, using the international 10 to 20 system. Specific neurofeedback training frequencies are associated with specific areas of the brain. Frequency band training enables an individual to self-regulate the activity of the brain, control the behavior, and observe improvements in the pre-existing health conditions. The following sections of this chapter will discuss the different forms of frequency band training and their applications in a clinical setting. (Marzbani et al., 2016)

Alpha Neurofeedback Training

Alpha waves of the brain are associated with alert relaxation and represent a calm and pleasant mood. The alpha waves exhibit creativity, which is associated with a state of relaxation. As alpha waves occur in the brain, the muscles of the body become relaxed. Meditation tends to increase the activity of alpha waves in the brain. At specific frequencies, the alpha waves are effective for the following disorders.

9 Hz alpha neurofeedback stimulation is useful for pain relief

10 and 30 Hz neurofeedback stimulation for alleviating stress and anxiety

10.2 Hz neurofeedback stimulation for treating brain injuries and improving memory and mental performance

7-10 Hz is the most common frequency bandwidth used in the alpha frequency neurofeedback training. This frequency range is associated with sleep, alleviation of stress and anxiety, and meditation. 10 Hz stimulation is used in deep muscle relaxation, regulating the rate of breathing, pain reduction, and heart rate reduction.

Beta Neurofeedback Training

Beta waves in the human brain demonstrate the mental performance of an individual. Inappropriate beta activity is indicative of physical and mental disorders that include ADHD, insomnia, and depression. Beta activity is associated with problem-solving abilities, conscious precision, and strong focus. At specific frequencies, the beta neurofeedback training is effective for the following functions.

12-14 Hz neurofeedback stimulation for improving attention and focus

7-9 Hz neurofeedback stimulation for improving the reading ability

14-22 Hz and 12-15 Hz neurofeedback stimulation for overthinking, OCD, cognitive processing, excessive worries, alcoholism, insomnia, and computational performance.

12-15 Hz neurofeedback stimulation for the reduction of stress, anxiety, anger, and epilepsy.

Beta frequency band training with relevant light and sound also improves the sleep cognitive performance while alleviating stress and fatigue.

Gamma Neurofeedback Training

Gamma waves are the highest frequency brain waves and are associated with memory and cognitive processing. Faster gamma waves are related to a faster speed of recalling memory. These fast rhythms determine the transfer of data from the brain to the outside world. Gamma waves are present in the hippocampus of the brain, which is responsible for the conversion of short-term memory to long-term memory. Gamma waves are also observed in spasms, seizures, and other sudden attacks. Gamma protocol in neurofeedback training is essential for problem-solving skills, mental sharpness, cognition, and brain activity.

Gamma frequency band training reduces the frequency of migraines attacks and increases information processing speed.

Delta Neurofeedback Training

The delta waves are observed in the third and fourth stages of sleep. These are the slowest brain waves and represent sleep, reduce pain, and increased comfort. Delta waves are used for the treatment of learning disorders, hard and sharp muscle contractions, headaches, and traumatic brain injury via 1-3 Hz stimulation. The delta waves eliminate worries or concerns as well as improve sleep.

Theta Neurofeedback Training

Theta waves of the brain are associated with emotion, sleep, memory, hypnosis, creativity, and meditation. The first stage of sleep also exhibits theta waves. Neurofeedback training with theta frequency is effective for the treatment of emotional disorders, ADHD, daydreaming, anxiety, depression, and distractibility.

Alpha/Theta Neurofeedback Training

Alpha/theta activity of the brain represents the distinction between sleep and awareness. This protocol of neurofeedback training is well known for its role in reducing stress. This form of neurofeedback training is also associated with addiction, depression, relaxation, anxiety, musical performance, trauma-related healing, and creativity. The frequency bandwidth for alpha/theta training is 7-8.5 Hz. During the treatment, auditory feedback is used while the therapy recipient keeps their eyes closed.

Conclusion

Neurofeedback training of the brain waves is associated with low and high frequencies. The low frequencies include alpha and theta waves.

Frequency band training with these waves improves focus and strengthens relaxation in the therapy recipients. The high-frequency brain waves include theta, beta, and low beta waves. Frequency band training with these waves stimulate organization, suppresses distraction, and improve activation of the training recipients.

Development of frequency band training

Overview of Neurofeedback Training

Neurofeedback is a form of biofeedback, characterized by the ability to consciously control the brain waves. During neurofeedback therapy, the brain waves are recorded using electroencephalography (EEG). The components of the EEG are extracted and demonstrated to the therapy recipients as audio, video, or both. During neurofeedback therapy, therapy recipients are capable of assessing the changes and their progress for optimum treatment performance. The recipients tend to improve their brain patterns in response to the assessed changes. Neurofeedback training of the brain waves is associated with low and high frequencies. The low frequencies include alpha and theta waves. Frequency band training with these waves improves focus and strengthen relaxation in the therapy recipients. The high-frequency brain waves include theta, beta, and low beta waves. Frequency band training with these waves stimulate organization, suppresses distraction, and improve activation of the training recipients. (Marzbani et al., 2016)

Ivan Pavlov

Ivan Pavlov laid the foundations of classical condition, which was followed by the first-ever description of the EEG in humans by Berger. The scientists and researchers observed that the alpha-blocking response on the human EEG can be classically conditioned. The alpha-blocking response involves the desynchronization of the alpha activity in the dominant hemisphere while the person has his or her eyes closed, into low voltage beta EEG. This alpha-blocking response fulfills the Pavlovian types of classical conditioning.

Dr. Joseph Kamiya

Dr. Joseph Kamiya performed one of the initial experiments in the field of neurofeedback training in the late 1960s. The basic neurofeedback design of this experiment was composed of two stages. The first stage, also known as the training session, included study subjects who assessed their mental state based on high or low alpha activity using the neurofeedback mechanisms. In the second stage, the study subjects were trained to enter into a state of high alpha activity when directed by an acoustic prompt. Kamiya concluded that 80% of the total study subjects were able to appreciate their mental state successfully and enter into the high alpha state when directed by an acoustic prompt.

Dr. Barry Sterman

Dr. Barry Sterman is known for the creation and establishment of clinical applications of neurofeedback training. During his research and experimentation, he discovered effective therapeutic approach for the treatment of different neurological conditions. He conducted training of the cat brains, using an experimental model similar to that of Pavlov's. On the acquisition of the desired rewards, the brains of the cats demonstrated sensorimotor frequency. The next part of the experiment required the cats to produce this brain frequency as a prerequisite for the acquisition of the reward. This experiment was the first to demonstrate and prove that brain waves can be modified using EEG conditioning and neurofeedback training.

Dr. Joel Lubar

Dr. Joel Lubar has contributed to the field of neurofeedback training for the treatment of ADHD. He reviewed Dr. Sterman's publications regarding neurofeedback training and epilepsy in 1972. He participated in a study that focused on the diagnosis of children with ADHD. The study demonstrated that neurofeedback training successfully alleviated or eliminated ADHD symptoms. This was accompanied by a substantial improvement in the executive functions of these children. Dr. Lubar developed his protocol for the treatment of ADHD by employing neurofeedback training. His protocol is a highly regarded method for the utilization of neurofeedback training in children and adults with ADHD.

Joe Kamiya: Beginnings of alpha training

Introduction

Alpha waves of the brain are associated with alert relaxation and represent a calm and pleasant mood. The alpha waves exhibit creativity, which is associated with a state of relaxation. As alpha waves occur in the brain, the muscles of the body become relaxed. Meditation tends to increase the activity of alpha waves in the brain. At specific frequencies, the alpha waves are effective for the following disorders.

9 Hz alpha neurofeedback stimulation is useful for pain relief

10 and 30 Hz neurofeedback stimulation for alleviating stress and anxiety

10.2 Hz neurofeedback stimulation for treating brain injuries and improving memory and mental performance

7-10 Hz is the most common frequency bandwidth used in the alpha frequency neurofeedback training. This frequency range is associated with sleep, alleviation of stress and anxiety, and meditation. 10 Hz stimulation is used in deep muscle relaxation, regulating the rate of breathing, pain reduction, and heart rate reduction. (Ossadtchi et al., 2017)

Discovery of Alpha Brain Waves

Joseph Kamiya conducted a discrimination experiment, which is part of the earliest studies related to neurofeedback training. After successfully conducting his experiment, he reported that human subjects of the experiment can efficiently distinguish between the alpha and non-alpha states. He also observed that human subjects who were trained for alpha discrimination demonstrated superior performance in tasks associated with the production of alpha waves.

Stages of Joe Kamiya's Study Design

The basic neurofeedback design of this experiment was composed of two stages. The first stage, also known as the training session, included study subjects who assessed their mental state based on high or low alpha activity using the neurofeedback mechanisms. In the second stage, the study subjects were trained to enter into a state of high alpha activity when directed by an acoustic prompt. Kamiya concluded that 80% of the total study subjects were able to appreciate their mental state successfully and enter into the high alpha state when directed by an acoustic prompt.

Alpha Waves and Neurofeedback Devices

Specific neurofeedback devices can be employed to stimulate the production and activity of the alpha waves in the brain. The device described in this section is a portable neurofeedback training device that comprises the EEG system, stimulates the activity of alpha waves in the brain, and enhances the memory of the device users. The portable wireless device also comprises a wireless low-energy Bluetooth, contiguous 5-minutes EEG power, and 1-second EEG power. The device successfully modulates alpha training and enhances both the working and episodic memory of the device users.

Elmer and Alyce Green: Alpha and theta training

Introduction to Alpha and Theta Training

Alpha/theta activity of the brain represents the distinction between sleep and awareness. This protocol of neurofeedback training is well known for its role in reducing stress. This form of neurofeedback training is also associated with addiction, depression, relaxation, anxiety, musical performance, trauma-related healing, and creativity. The frequency bandwidth for alpha/theta training is 7-8.5 Hz. During the treatment, auditory feedback is used while the therapy recipient keeps their eyes closed.

Development of Clinical Biofeedback by Elmer and Alyce Green

Elmer and Alyce Green are visionary authors, teachers, and researchers who combined wisdom traditions and scientific exploration strategies to give rise to the field of clinical biofeedback. The researchers also enabled numerous individuals to learn self-regulation and self-awareness by undergoing biofeedback and neurofeedback training offered by trained individuals. The Greens also represented that ordinary individuals can gain voluntary control over their physiologic functions, which are otherwise involuntary in normal circumstances. These physiologic functions comprise the brain waves, heart rate, blood flow, temperature, muscle tension, and blood pressure. The Greens are accredited for the discovery of the association between skin temperature feedback and the treatment of migraines. They also developed a biofeedback protocol for the treatment and management of hypertension. They also studied the voluntary control of the yogis over their physiologic functions in the 1970s. Their work was documented in a film called Biofeedback: The Yoga of the West.

Visualization and Creativity

A visualization feedback protocol is employed for the training of brain waves using motor imagery. The brain-computer interface helps individuals in modulating the electrical activity of their brain to achieve a predetermined therapeutic or experimental goal. The visualization feedback protocol reflects the distribution of EEG and electrical activity of the brain in real-time. The diffusion map process translates the EEG evaluation into visual feedback. The selection of an optimal frequency band also plays an important role in the visualization feedback protocol for the motor imagery-based training of the brain waves. (Ossadtchi et al., 2017)

Alpha-Theta-Training

Overview of Alpha-Theta Training

Alpha/theta activity of the brain represents the distinction between sleep and awareness. This protocol of neurofeedback training is well known for its role in reducing stress. This form of neurofeedback training is also associated with addiction, depression, relaxation, anxiety, musical performance, trauma-related healing, and creativity. The frequency bandwidth for alpha/theta training is 7-8.5 Hz. During the treatment, auditory feedback is used while the therapy recipient keeps their eyes closed.

The Deep States in Alpha-Theta Training

Learning associated with the alpha-theta training takes place during the twilight state of the sleep-wake cycle. When an individual is awake, the activity of the beta waves is predominantly higher. These brain waveforms enable an individual to focus on the given tasks throughout the day. However, at the night, the delta brain waveforms or sleep waves predominate. As the day goes by, the electrical activity of the brain of a person transforms from beta, alpha, theta, and ultimately delta brain waveforms as the night approaches. Alpha waves serve as a transition between the theta and beta waves, thus, connecting the subconscious internal world of a person with his or her external world. Alpha-theta training of the brain waves elicits hypnagogic imagery, which provides them with more in-depth insight into their life experiences. The reinforcement of alpha waves is approximately 50-70% whereas the reinforcement of theta waves is approximately 20-50% in the alpha-theta training. The deep state of consciousness is associated with a decrease in the amplitude of alpha waves and an increase in the amplitude of the theta waves.

Alpha-Theta Treatment Protocol

Alpha/theta activity of the brain represents the distinction between sleep and awareness. This protocol of neurofeedback training is well known for its role in reducing stress. This form of neurofeedback training is also associated with addiction, depression, relaxation, anxiety, musical performance, trauma-related healing, and creativity. The frequency bandwidth for alpha/theta training is 7-8.5 Hz. During the treatment, auditory feedback is used while the therapy recipient keeps their eyes closed. Other treatment protocols include alpha synchrony training and alpha enhancement training of the brain waves. (Ossadtchi et al., 2017)

Sensory Placement in Alpha-Theta Training

Sensory placement in the alpha-theta training always occurs on the posterior aspects of the head. The levels of alpha and theta brain activities are compared across the two cerebral hemispheres. Some important points related to the assessment of alpha and theta waves in the alpha-theta training are listed down below.

When P3>P4, the brain waves are trained to increase either P4 or O2.

When alpha waves are symmetrical but P4 is greater than P3, brain waves are trained at O1.

When P4>P3 for the alpha waves but P3=P4 for the theta waves, the brain waves are trained at Pz.

Contraindications of Alpha-Theta Training

The contraindications of alpha-theta training are listed as follows.

Alpha-theta is contraindicated in patients with ADHD as there is widespread slowing of the EEG.

Individuals who are anxious and have excessive alpha activity at the posterior aspect are recommended not to undergo alpha-theta training of the brain waves.

Alpha-theta training is also contraindicated in trauma who have dissociated. This is because the eyes are required to remain open during the theta oppression, and the patients shall practice grounding before the initiation of alpha-theta training of the brain waves.

The placement of P3 sensors is contraindication in individuals who are suffering from depression.

Barry Sterman: The discovery of SMR training and epilepsy

Barry Sterman's Experiment

During his research and experimentation, Barry Sterman discovered an effective therapeutic approach for the treatment of several neurological conditions. He conducted an experiment on the cats, contrary to his use of dogs by Pavlov, and used an experimental model similar to that of Pavlov. On the acquisition of the desired rewards, the brains of the cats demonstrated sensorimotor frequency. The next part of the experiment required the cats to produce this brain frequency as a prerequisite for the acquisition of the reward. This experiment was the first to demonstrate and prove that brain waves can be modified using EEG conditioning and neurofeedback training. (Alqahtani et al., 2020)

SMR Neurofeedback Training

The SMR neurofeedback training protocol comprises the thalamocortical loops of the brain and counters the interference of the processing of the somatosensory information, which can occur in the presence of motor activity. This may otherwise lead to a decline in the cognitive performance of an individual. SMR is a component of the alpha rhythm of the brain, and the SMR neurofeedback training facilitates the greater integration and processing of somatosensory information in the brain. SMR neurofeedback training protocol is also effective for improving attention, perception, and semantic working memory. It enhances cognitive functioning in older individuals. (Morales-Quezada et al., 2019)

Neurofeedback Training for Epilepsy

Epilepsy-specific medications are clinically ineffective in a significant percentage of epilepsy patients. Effective treatment for such patients is neurofeedback training. Reduced slow rhythms with a frequency range of 4-7 Hz and increased SMR with a frequency range of 12-15 Hz are diagnostic characteristics of epilepsy. Continuous SMR treatment in epilepsy patients modulates uncontrolled epilepsy and lowers the rate of seizures.

Joel Lubar: SMR and Theta-Beta Training in Attention Deficit Disorder

Theta-Beta Neurofeedback Training

Theta-beta neurofeedback training works by decreasing the theta/beta ratio in the brain. The ratio has inverse relationship with the executive cognitive control, therefore, the theta-beta neurofeedback training is an important tool for improving the cognitive and overall human performance. Neurofeedback training helps the individuals gain greater control over the electrical activity of the brain and increase and decrease the amplitudes of the target brain waves.

Joel Lubar and Theta-Beta Training

Dr. Joel Lubar has contributed significantly to the treatment of ADHD via neurofeedback training. He reviewed Dr. Sterman's publications regarding neurofeedback training and epilepsy in 1972. He participated in a study that focused on the diagnosis of children with ADHD. The study demonstrated that neurofeedback training successfully alleviated or eliminated ADHD symptoms. This was accompanied by a substantial improvement in the executive functions of these children. Dr. Lubar developed his protocol for the treatment of ADHD by employing theta-beta neurofeedback training. His protocol is a highly regarded method for the utilization of theta-beta neurofeedback training in children and adults with ADHD.

Attention-Deficit Hyperactivity Disorder

Overview

Attention-deficit hyperactivity disorder or ADHD is referred to as a psychiatric condition, which impairs the functional abilities of an individual. Individuals with ADHD demonstrate patterns of hyperactivity, impulsivity, or inattentiveness. The three subtypes of ADHD include predominantly hyperactive, predominantly inattentive, and combined ADHD type characterized by both hyperactivity and inattentiveness. The symptoms of ADHD appear at an early age during childhood. The ADHD symptoms include disorganization, lack of concentration, forgetfulness, lack of attention, losing objects, and difficulty in completing the assigned tasks. In order for the psychiatric condition to be labeled as ADHD, the symptoms must appear before the child turns 12 years old, persisted for a period of six months, and hinder the routine activities of the child. The symptoms of ADHD appear at multiple settings, such as at home and at school. This psychiatric condition may have serious consequences such as abnormal and unhealthy social interactions, difficulty in achieving goals at school and community, increased demonstration of risky behaviors, and the jobs and professional conduct is at stake for individuals with ADHD. In relation to the anatomy of the human brain, ADHD is associated with dysfunction of the frontal lobe of the cerebral cortex, manifest as impaired executive functioning of the affected individual. In addition to inattentiveness, hyperactivity, and impulsivity, children with ADHD face difficulties in emotional regulation and making both significant and non-significant decisions. Children suffering from ADHD face challenges during social interactions, they become irritable and easily frustrated, and demonstrate impulsive behaviors. Owing to these signs and symptoms, these children are usually named as troublemakers.

Etiological Basis of ADHD

ADHD is a result of interaction between both genetic and environmental factors. When it comes to psychiatric health conditions, ADHD is among the most heritable conditions. The incidence and prevalence of ADHD are relatively greater in monozygotic twins than in dizygotic twins. As compared to the general population, siblings are at a greater risk of developing this psychiatric condition. Environmental factors associated with ADHD include smoking, viral infections, exposure of the fetus to alcohol during pregnancy, exposure of the fetus to tobacco smoke during pregnancy, and deficiency of nutrients is responsible for the onset of ADHD. Individuals with ADHD exhibit a lesser number of dopamine receptors in the frontal lobe of the brain. Hence, these receptors are also associated with the onset of ADHD in these individuals. The researchers and scientists have also discovered and elaborated on the role of involvement of nor adrenergic receptors in the development of this psychiatric condition. (Alqahtani et al., 2020)

Epidemiology of ADHD

The three subtypes of ADHD – predominantly inattentive ADHD, predominantly hyperactive ADHD, and combined type ADHD – have different patterns of prevalence. Of the total number of ADHD patients, 18.3% of individuals suffer from inattentive subtype ADHD and 8.3% of individuals suffer from hyperactive or impulsive subtype ADHD. In contrast to this, 70% of the total individuals with ADHD suffer from combined type ADHD, making this ADHD more prevalent than the other two subtypes. Moreover, the inattentive subtype of ADHD is more prevalent in the female population than in the male population. However, the collective prevalence of all the ADHD subtypes has a prevalence male to female ratio of 2 to 1. The total prevalence of ADHD in the adult population is approximately 3-6%. This psychiatric condition is the most prevalent psychiatric condition in the pediatric population. Research evidence also demonstrates that the prevalence of ADHD is relatively greater in the United States than in the other developed regions of the world.

Pathophysiology of ADHD

The signs and symptoms of ADHD – hyperactivity, inattentiveness, impulsivity, forgetfulness, difficulty in decision-making, difficulty in completing the assigned tasks, abnormal and unhealthy social interactions, and difficulties in professional life as well as the demonstration of risky behaviors – are associated with cognitive and functional deficits in the human brain. These deficits arise due to diffuse abnormalities in the human brain. There is a decrease in the size and volume of the dorsolateral prefrontal cortex as well as the anterior cingulate gyrus in the brains of individuals with ADHD. These volume and size changes are responsible for causing goal-directed behavior deficits in individuals suffering from ADHD. The fMRI measuring the functional activity of the brain demonstrates decreased activity in the frontostriatal region of the brain in individuals suffering from this psychiatric condition. Adequate understanding of the pathophysiological mechanisms is important for the development of pharmacologic and other therapeutic interventions for the treatment of ADHD. One shall note that there are not any standard imaging findings or laboratory evaluations particularly curated for individuals with ADHD.

Diagnosis and Clinical Evaluation of ADHD

The diagnosis of ADHD largely depends on taking the relevant history of individuals suffering from ADHD. Children are diagnosed with this psychiatric condition based on clinical history and because of symptoms according to the given diagnostic guideline. The inattentive symptoms of ADHD include the following.

Lack of adequate attention to tasks

Ignoring or missing out on minor details related to the assigned task

Rushing the assigned tasks and not giving enough attention to them

Not paying attention to or listening to when the teacher, parent, or some other person is assigning tasks and giving out instruction

Facing difficulties during tasks that require the application of organizational skills

Not completing the assigned tasks

Avoiding and demonstrating dislike for tasks that require persistent mental efforts and attention

Constantly losing or misplacing objects

Being forgetful of both significant and non-significant details

The symptoms of hyperactivity in ADHD are listed down below.

Fidgeting with objects

Leaving the seat persistently after short periods

Climbing on objects

Having a loud voice or talking loudly

Blurting out answers in the classroom or in a social interaction

Excessive talking and talking or answering questions even if it is not the individual's turn

Find it difficult to wait for the turn

Interrupt others while they are speaking or doing an activity or intrude while others are interacting

Both the symptoms of the hyperactivity subtype of ADHD and the inattentive subtype of ADHD shall be present in more than one setting. Multiple settings may include home, school, social gatherings, workplace, and other settings. The above-mentioned core symptoms of hyperactivity and inattentiveness in ADHD are not present in adults with ADHD. Rather, these symptoms are replaced by other relevant problems that include instability of the mood, procrastination, and having a low self-esteem. Adults diagnosed with ADHD tend to more inattentive and impulsive in nature. In contrast to this, individuals with hyperactivity subtype of ADHD are better able to manage their hyperactivity symptoms. While taking the relevant history of a child with ADHD, the symptoms of hyperactivity and inattentiveness may either be missed or elicited during the process.

This psychiatric condition interferes with the executive functioning and the developmental pattern of an individual. Adults are also affected by the complications in ADHD and find it difficult to carry out the routine activities in a normal way. It is important to consider different life events, routine activities, and the difficulties and challenges that the patient report to make a correct diagnosis. Different scales have been developed by the researchers, scientists, and healthcare providers to measure the challenges and problems that the individuals with ADHD encounter in their daily, academic, social, personal, and professional life activities. One of the scales used to measure these problems is called the Brown Attention Deficit Disorder Scale. This scale is used for the identification of ADHD in the adult male and female population. The scale includes a range of common areas, related to which the difficulties are encountered by the ADHD patient. The Vanderbilt ADHD Scale is also a measurement and assessment tool, which is used for the identification of ADHD in the pediatric population. This scale also contains both parent and teacher components to facilitate the identification and diagnosis of ADHD in children. Unlike other health and psychiatric conditions, the physical examination does not contribute significantly to the identification and diagnosis of ADHD in both the pediatric and adult populations. However, physical examination is a useful tool for the exclusion of other pathological conditions that may be responsible for the symptoms, mentioned in the preceding paragraph. These medical conditions may include thyroid problems. Physical examination is also useful for the identification and diagnosis of other medical or health conditions, which facilitate the treatment plan. This can be elaborated by the example that individuals suffering from hypertension shall not opt for stimulants as a pharmacological therapeutic approach for the treatment and management of the symptoms of ADHD.

The diagnosis of ADHD is almost entirely clinical and is based on the relevant history of the individual suffering from ADHD. The diagnosis of ADHD is not associated with any specific radiologic imaging findings or lab evaluations. The clinical evaluation of individuals suffering from ADHD is usually done using different rating scales, two of which have already been described in the previous paragraph. The multiple informants involved in the diagnosis of ADHD may include the parents and teachers of the child suffering from ADHD. The clinician also assesses the presence of any other medical condition, which may be responsible for the relevant signs and symptoms. The types of ADHD according to the DSM 5 are listed down below.

Predominantly impulsive or hyperactive subtype of ADHD

Predominantly inattentive subtype of ADHD

Combination subtype of ADHD that includes both inattentiveness and hyperactivity

The diagnostic criteria for ADHD also require that the onset of the above-mentioned symptoms shall occur before the child turns 12 years old, the symptoms shall be present in multiple settings such as home, workplace, school, and social gatherings, and the psychiatric condition shall produce significant impairment in the academic performance, social interactions, and occupational functioning of the affected individual, and that the psychiatric condition shall not be associated with the symptoms of any other psychiatric or behavioral disorder.

Treatment of ADHD

Before discussing the neurofeedback training for the treatment and management of the symptoms of ADHD, one shall acquire a thorough understanding of the conventional pharmacological therapeutic approaches and other treatment modalities relevant to ADHD in both children and adults. Pharmacological therapy is the standard treatment modality for individuals suffering from this psychiatric condition. The two major categories of pharmacological formulations include stimulant medications and non-stimulant medications. The stimulant medications further comprise methylphenidates and amphetamines. These stimulants work by blocking the reuptake of a neurotransmitter called dopamine at the level of both presynaptic membranes and postsynaptic membranes. In addition to this, amphetamines also release this neurotransmitter directly into the synaptic cleft. Stimulants demonstrate effectiveness in managing and reducing the symptoms of ADHD in approximately 70% of the total individuals suffering from this psychiatric condition. (Magnus, 2022)

Different formulations are available for the two stimulant medications. These formulations include immediate-release and extended-release or sustained-release formulations. The adverse effects associated with the use of stimulant medications include a decrease in appetite, reduced sleep, changes in blood pressure, and an increased risk of dependency on stimulant medications. Individuals suffering from ADHD are vulnerable to substance abuse. The intake of stimulant medications significantly reduces the risk for the development of lifetime dependency and substance abuse. Recent studies demonstrate that the use of stimulants is considered for those who are suffering from epilepsy. The addition of alpha-agonist pharmacological formulation in the treatment regimen may help with the treatment and management of tic disorders alongside the treatment and management of ADHD.

The non-stimulant medications used for the treatment and management of ADHD include alpha-agonists and antidepressant medications. In the category of antidepressant medications, the best-known drug is atomoxetine. This drug is a selective norepinephrine reuptake inhibitor. The drug has been effective in several drug trials as an effective option for the treatment of ADHD. However, antidepressant medications are not as effective as stimulant medications are. Atomoxetine has lesser antidepressant effects. These medications are often prescribed to children who are either suffering from anxiety or can't tolerate the stimulant medications for the treatment of ADHD. Antidepressant medications also include bupropion. This medication is associated with the neurotransmitters – serotonin and dopamine. In the alpha-agonists category of medications for the treatment and management of ADHD, guanfacine and clonidine are effective pharmacologic formulations. However, these medications are associated with several adverse effects that include a decrease in blood pressure, an increase in weight, dizziness, and sedation. Sedation is relatively observed with the intake of clonidine than with the intake of guanfacine. Moreover, alpha-agonist medications are more effective in the younger pediatric population rather than the adult population. (Magnus, 2022)

In addition to pharmacological treatment and management of ADHD using stimulant and non-stimulant medications, psychological treatment is also an important therapeutic approach for the treatment of this psychiatric condition. The psychological therapeutic measures for individuals with ADHD are listed down below.

Providing psychological education to both the patient and the patient's family

Induction of cognitive-behavioral training programs for individuals with ADHD to discuss and facilitate the patient in achieving the short-term and long-term treatment and management goals.

These training programs are effective when they are used with the intake of relevant medications for the treatment and management of ADHD. However, in contrast to other psychiatric conditions, pharmacological treatment and interventions without the use of psychological therapy are most effective for the management and treatment of ADHD. In addition to this, the Food and Drug Administration or FDA has approved the use of a trigeminal nerve stimulation system for the treatment of ADHD in children who are not consuming any medications. This stimulation device produces a low-level electrical pulse that inhibits hyperactivity, alleviating the relevant symptoms. The research studies and clinical investigations that are done so far have not found a significant association between the role of diet in the treatment and management of ADHD and the related symptoms.

Prognosis of ADHD

The prognosis and treatment outcomes of ADHD depend on different factors. These factors include the age of the individual diagnosed with ADHD, the presence of other psychiatric and physical health conditions, and the treatment measures undertaken for the management of symptoms. Despite its diagnosis in the childhood stage of an individual, the symptoms of ADHD may persist even if the child grows into a teenager or adolescent. These symptoms may influence both the academic and social aspects of the teenage life of an individual. A quarter of these individuals may also suffer from the concurrent antisocial disorder. However, the symptoms of ADHD reduce as an adolescent enters the adulthood stage of life. It is estimated that 50% of individuals with ADHD tend to grow out of ADHD as they grow into adults. 25% of the individuals do not require treatment for the management of symptoms of ADHD. The factors responsible for this trend are listed down below.

The development of the frontal lobe of the brain improves upon the intake of stimulant medications

The adults may choose career pathways that do not demand sustained attention

As these individuals grow into adults, they become capable of achieving their goals, both social, academic, and professional. The psychological and pharmacological treatments of ADHD are also important for improving the symptoms of conduct disorder and oppositional defiant disorder. The treatment also reduces the risk of substance abuse in the patients. Individuals with ADHD who remain untreated for this psychiatric disorder may experience devastating consequences and persistent dysfunction when carrying out routine tasks.

Theta-Beta Training for ADHD

Individuals with ADHD often demonstrate the symptoms of hyperactivity and impulsivity. These symptoms are associated with increase in the theta/beta ratio. Individuals with ADHD demonstrate low arousal levels in the frontal lobe of the cerebral cortex, owing to excess of theta waves and concomitant deficit of beta waves. Neurofeedback training of the brain can enable individuals with ADHD to increase their beta activity and decrease theta activity, leading to an increase in the level of arousal in the frontal lobe of the cerebral cortex. Neurofeedback training for the treatment and management of ADHD involves the placement of electrodes over the scalp surface, to monitor the electrical activity of the brain. The patients are provided with feedback in the form of audio or visual signals. After the patient is trained for stimulating the appropriate electrical activity in the brain, a reduction in impulsive and hyperactive symptoms is observed.

Theta-beta neurofeedback training alleviates the symptoms of ADHD, hyperactivity, and impulsivity.

Randomized controlled trails demonstrate that approximately 30-40 sessions of theta-beta neurofeedback training has comparable efficacy with methylphenidate in alleviating the hyperactivity and inattentive symptoms of ADHD. The outcomes and efficacy of theta-beta training are evident by the fact that neurofeedback training equips individuals diagnosed with ADHD, the ability to self-regulate their attention and functional activity. In addition to theta-beta neurofeedback training for the treatment and management of ADHD, SMR neurofeedback training is also effective for reduction in the symptoms of ADHD. Studies also reveal that the hyperactivity-reducing effects of both SMR and theta-beta neurofeedback trainings persist even after the stimulant medications are withdrawn in these children. (Van Doren et al., 2018)

Vincent Monastra: The Theta-Beta Quotient

Neurofeedback for ADHD

rece

Different neurofeedback training protocols are used for the treatment of children and adults with ADHD.

SMR Enhancement/Theta Suppression

SMR enhancement/theta suppression is a form of EEG biofeedback training that facilitates individuals with ADHD to gain control over impulsive and hyperactive behaviors by increasing SMR production at either C3 or C4 as well as decreasing the production of theta waves simultaneously. In response to the neurofeedback training, the patient receives auditory and visual feedback.

SMR Enhancement/Beta-2 Suppression

The second treatment protocol for ADHD treatment is called SMR enhancement/beta-2 suppression. This is secondary SMR training. The predominantly hyperactive-impulsive types of ADHD patients for increasing their SMR activity and decreasing their beta-2 activity at the same time. This involves the recording of the electrical activity of the brain at the C4 site. Individuals suffering combined type ADHD also receive this neurofeedback training for half of the treatment duration. In the other half, the theta suppression/beta-1 enhancement neurofeedback training protocol is utilized.

Theta Suppression/Beta-1 Enhancement

The third protocol for individuals with ADHD, theta suppression/beta-1 enhancement, involves training ADHD patients for increasing the production of beta-1 waves and suppressing the production of theta-1 waves at the same time. The site where the recordings of the electrical activity of the brain are recorded is Cz. Individuals with predominantly inattentive type ADHD are subjected to theta suppression/beta-1 enhancement neurofeedback training at site C3. Feedback is provided upon successful control of the theta or beta waves of the brain. (Van Doren et al., 2018)

Theta-Beta Ratio for Cognitive Processing

As mentioned in the previous chapter, the theta/beta ratio is in inverse relationship with the cognitive function of an individual. Increased theta/beta ratio in individuals with ADHD is associated with the onset of the related symptoms and impairment of cognitive functions. Theta-beta neurofeedback training reduces this ratio and optimizes the cognitive functions in individuals with ADHD while alleviating the symptoms.

Theta-Beta Marker for ADHD

The theta-beta ratio or theta-beta EEG power ratio is approved by the Food and Drugs Administration as a diagnostic marker in individuals with ADHD.

Hödlmoser: SMR training and sleep

Sleep and Brain Activity

The sleep-wake cycle comprises four cycles of sleep. Stage I sleep is characterized by a state of drowsiness, stage II sleep is described as light sleep during which the frequency and amplitude of EEG waves decrease and increase respectively. During this stage of sleep, there is a high-frequency spike in the sleep spindles. Stage III sleep is characterized by moderate to deep sleep, during which the sleep spindles decrease in number and the amplitude of waves with low-frequency increases. Stage IV sleep is the deepest stage of sleep characterized by delta waves, which are high-amplitude and low-frequency waves. These four stages of sleep are non-rapid eye movement (non-REM) sleep and are followed by the occurrence of REM sleep. In REM sleep, the activity of the brain represents an alert and wakeful state.

Importance of Sleep Spindles for Memory Performance

Sleep spindles are integral to the process of neuroplasticity and consolidation of memory. The sleep spindles propagate from the anterior to the posterior part of the cerebral cortex. The sleep spindles on EEG are a hallmark of the NREM stages of sleep.

SMR Training and Sleep

SMR neurofeedback training improves both declarative memory and sleep. The SMR enhancement is associated with changes in the sleep spindles and consolidation of memory during the night. The training protocol induces a beneficial effect on the cognition of the training recipients. SMR neurofeedback training protocol is a non-invasive and non-pharmacological therapeutic approach for enhancing the quality of sleep.

Kerstin Hödlmoser's Study Design

Kerstin Hödlmoser conducted an experiment to test her hypothesis regarding the association between memory consolidation processes and increases in the spindle activity of non-REM sleep after learning. She also investigated the relationship of sleep traits with cognition, spindle activity, and learning in children. The experiment included prepubertal healthy children who were subjected to ambulatory polysomnography for two nights. Hödlmoser and other authors assessed the effects of non-learning and prior learning on the activity of the sleep spindles of the brain.

Study Outcomes

The experiment revealed some important findings. Firstly, the sleep spindles peaked in the slow sleep spindle frequency range. Children who demonstrated greater sleep spindle activity at the frontal, occipital, parietal, and central sites also demonstrated greater levels of cognitive functioning and declarative memory.

3.1.9 Davidson and Rosenfeld: Alpha training in depression

Overview of Alpha Training

Alpha neurofeedback training is associated with sleep, alleviation of stress and anxiety, and meditation. 7-10 Hz is the most common frequency bandwidth used in the alpha frequency neurofeedback training. 10 Hz stimulation is used in deep muscle relaxation, regulating the rate of breathing, pain reduction, and heart rate reduction. (EK;Frey, 2016)

Alpha Asymmetry Neurofeedback Protocol

Frontal alpha asymmetry in the alpha neurofeedback training is associated with the emotional and motivational responses. Frontal asymmetry describes the average activity of the right and left frontal regions of the brain. Frontal asymmetry including the greater activity of the left frontal lobe indicates greater emotional flexibility, improved emotional regulation, and decreased negative effects. Extreme asymmetry at the right frontal lobe of the brain is associated with depression and other affective disorders.

Alpha Training for Depression

Asymmetrical neurofeedback training of the right frontal lobe of the brain increases the activity of the alpha brain waves and has greater positive effects on the emotional and cognitive functioning of the training recipients. Asymmetry neurofeedback training also improves the functions of the left frontal lobe, and collectively alleviates the symptoms of depression.

Hammond: Beta-SMR Training in Depression

D. Corydon Hammond

D. Corydon Hammond is a renowned psychologist who described the effects of beta-SMR training in the treatment of depression. He used neurofeedback training protocols, comprising beta and SMR training, for the treatment of depression.

Roshi's Light Stimulation and Left Hemisphere Beta Training

ROSHI is a neurofeedback training device, which is used for the treatment of depression. Roshi light stimulation combines both neurofeedback training and photic stimulation to induce beta training of the left hemisphere of the brain. After several sessions with Roshi light stimulation, the patients report alleviation in the symptoms of depression and an increase in their energy levels.

Technical background

Neurophysiological Basis of EEG

The EEG recordings demonstrate the electrical activity of the brain, which corresponds to the electrical activity of similarly oriented neurons in the cerebral cortex. These electric signals are net inhibitory and excitatory potentials generated by the cerebral cortical neurons.

Amplifier and Sensor Materials in EEG

EEG uses high impedance amplifiers which conduct the electrical charges from the surface electrodes. However, these amplifiers do not permit optimal spatial resolution. Trans-impedance amplifiers keep the surface electrodes at the reference potential or ground and permit the optimal spatial resolution of the EEG signals. EEG uses both dry electrodes and electrodes which require the prior application of salt and gel over the surface of the scalp. The dry electrodes further comprise hybrid dry sensors and dry fabric-based sensors.

EEG Sampling and Processing

Adequate sampling and processing rates are crucial to the assessment of fast and slow brain wave activities. For high-frequency EEG waves, higher sampling rates are required. The range of sampling rates is 250-2000 Hz. Different EEG and neurofeedback training systems require different sampling and processing measures.

Components of EEG

The components of EEG include an EEG system comprising a monitor and processor, surface electrodes, an amplifier, and salt or gels to promote electrical conductivity of the scalp.

LORETA Neurofeedback

LORETA is an inverse solution technique, which estimates the origin of electrical signals by developing an electrode grid over the surface of the scalp. LORETA z-score neurofeedback training, also called LORETA ZNFB is an important therapeutic approach that involves neurofeedback training of deeper sources of electrical signals.

Practical procedure

Consultation with the Physician

Similar to other medical procedures, neurofeedback training also requires thorough consultation with the physician prior to the neurofeedback training procedure. The initial appointment with the physician usually involves a detailed discussion of the previous history of the patient, objectives of the neurofeedback training, underlying pathophysiology, and the expectations of the patient under consideration. Consultation with the physician also includes the discussion about frequency band training and the estimated number of training sessions required for the therapy. The form of neurofeedback training and the target brain waveform is also determined before the initiation of the neurofeedback therapy. The physician shall also ensure that the patient is the right candidate for neurofeedback training and does not have any relative contraindications or exposed wounds of the skull.

Q-EEG Assessment

Quantitative electroencephalography (QEEG), also known as the modern EEG analysis, is described as the recording of digital EEG signals. Complex mathematical algorithms are used to process, transform, and analyze these EEG signals. The new techniques associated with QEEG include the analysis of signal complexity and specific frequency band, network analysis, and analysis of connectivity. The clinical significance of QEEG evaluation is implied in epilepsy, stroke, traumatic brain injury, dementia, mental health disorders, and neuropsychiatric disorders. QEEG provides additional insight to the diagnosis of clinical ailments to acquire precise diagnosis, accurate assessment of the disease severity, and evaluation of the specific treatment response.

Clinical Applications of Q-EEG Scan

The clinical applications of the QEEG scan include the screening of potential seizures, screening of the epileptic seizures, pre-surgical assessment of individuals with drug-resistant epilepsy, identification of acute onset intraoperative intracranial complications, ambulatory EEG, and assessment of the severity of the encephalopathies and dementia. QEEG provides differential diagnoses for the different subtypes of epileptic seizures. Different seizure subtypes are characterized by a different pattern on the QEEG scan, hence, providing an efficient diagnosis of epileptic seizures. The delta/alpha ratio and theta/beta ratio in the QEEG assessment play an important role in the diagnosis and monitoring of stroke patients. The Brain Symmetry Index is used for the measurement of ischemic damage to the brain. The Brain Function Index (BFI) in QEEG assessment is a quantitative marker for assessing the impairment of brain function in individuals suffering from traumatic brain injury. QEEG is in combination with conventional EEG recording to analyze carotid endarterectomy, disrupted cerebral blood flow, and cerebrovascular interventions in the setting of intensive care units. QEEG also serves as a useful diagnostic tool for learning and attention disorders. It is effective for different diagnoses in severe morphological or physiological changes vs minimal changes associated with depression.

Neurofeedback Therapy

After going through all the chapters of this book, you will acquire a greater understanding of the electrical activity of the brain and how it can be utilized in neurofeedback training to facilitate the treatment, management, and diagnosis of various health conditions. Neurofeedback therapy is a cost-effective and non-invasive approach that is performed by trained and experienced EEG technicians or technologists, using the EEG system, electrodes, salts and gels, and an amplifier. Various forms of neurofeedback therapy are available along with different types of treatment protocols, each of which is specifically tailored for a certain region of the brain with a particular function.

Bibliography

Van Doren, J., Arns, M., Heinrich, H., Vollebregt, M. A., Strehl, U., & K. Loo, S. (2018). Sustained effects of neurofeedback in ADHD: a systematic review and meta-analysis. European Child & Adolescent Psychiatry, 28(3), 293–305. https://doi.org/10.1007/s00787-018-1121-4

Magnus. (2022, May 8). Attention Deficit Hyperactivity Disorder. https://pubmed.ncbi.nlm.nih.gov/28722868/

Alqahtani, F., Imran, I., Pervaiz, H., Ashraf, W., Perveen, N., Rasool, M. F., Alasmari, A. F., Alharbi, M., Samad, N., Alqarni, S. A., Al-Rejaie, S. S., & Alanazi, M. M. (2020). Non-pharmacological Interventions for Intractable Epilepsy. Saudi Pharmaceutical Journal, 28(8), 951–962. https://doi.org/10.1016/j.jsps.2020.06.016

Morales-Quezada, L., Martinez, D., El-Hagrassy, M. M., Kaptchuk, T. J., Sterman, M. B., & Yeh, G. Y. (2019). Neurofeedback impacts cognition and quality of life in pediatric focal epilepsy: An exploratory randomized double-blinded sham-controlled trial. Epilepsy & Behavior, 101, 106570. https://doi.org/10.1016/j.yebeh.2019.106570

Ossadtchi, A., Shamaeva, T., Okorokova, E., Moiseeva, V., & Lebedev, M. A. (2017). Neurofeedback learning modifies the incidence rate of alpha spindles, but not their duration and amplitude. Scientific Reports, 7(1). https://doi.org/10.1038/s41598-017-04012-0

Nan, W., Dias, A. P. B., & Rosa, A. C. (2019). Neurofeedback Training for Cognitive and Motor Function Rehabilitation in Chronic Stroke: Two Case Reports. Frontiers in Neurology, 10. https://doi.org/10.3389/fneur.2019.00800

Kober, S. E., Schweiger, D., Reichert, J. L., Neuper, C., & Wood, G. (2017). Upper Alpha Based Neurofeedback Training in Chronic Stroke: Brain Plasticity Processes and Cognitive Effects. Applied Psychophysiology and Biofeedback, 42(1), 69–83. https://doi.org/10.1007/s10484-017-9353-5

Wang, T., Mantini, D., & Gillebert, C. R. (2018). The potential of real-time fMRI neurofeedback for stroke rehabilitation: A systematic review. Cortex, 107, 148–165. https://doi.org/10.1016/j.cortex.2017.09.006

Rehman, I., Navid Mahabadi, Sanvictores, T., & Rehman, C. I. (2021, August 27). Classical Conditioning. Nih.gov; StatPearls Publishing. https://www.ncbi.nlm.nih.gov/books/NBK470326/

Rehman. (2021, August 27). Classical Conditioning. https://pubmed.ncbi.nlm.nih.gov/29262194/

Staddon, J. E. R., & Cerutti, D. T. (2003). Operant Conditioning. Annual Review of Psychology, 54(1), 115–144. https://doi.org/10.1146/annurev.psych.54.101601.145124

Gandhi, M. H., & Mukherji, P. (2021, July 22). Learning Theories. Nih.gov; StatPearls Publishing. https://www.ncbi.nlm.nih.gov/books/NBK562189/

Badyal, D., & Singh, T. (2017). Learning theories: The basics to learn in medical education. International Journal of Applied and Basic Medical Research, 7(5), 1. https://doi.org/10.4103/ijabmr.ijabmr_385_17

EK;Frey, L. (2016). Electroencephalography (EEG): An Introductory Text and Atlas of Normal and Abnormal Findings in Adults, Children, and Infants [Internet]. https://pubmed.ncbi.nlm.nih.gov/27748095/

Biasiucci, A., Franceschiello, B., & Murray, M. M. (2019). Electroencephalography. Current Biology, 29(3), R80–R85. https://doi.org/10.1016/j.cub.2018.11.052

Enache AL;Slujitoru AS;Pintea IL;Stocheci CM;Mateescu GO;Gheorghişor I. (2012). Histological and immunohistochemical aspects of cerebral vessels of the elderly. Romanian Journal of Morphology and Embryology = Revue Roumaine de Morphologie et Embryologie, 53(4). https://pubmed.ncbi.nlm.nih.gov/23303030/

Dayan, A. D. (1970). Quantitative histological studies on the aged human brain. Acta Neuropathologica, 16(2), 85–94. https://doi.org/10.1007/bf00687663

Jeans, A., & Esiri, M. (2008). Brain histology. Practical Neurology, 8(5), 303–310. https://doi.org/10.1136/jnnp.2008.156893

Herbet, G., & Duffau, H. (2020). Revisiting the Functional Anatomy of the Human Brain: Toward a Meta-Networking Theory of Cerebral Functions. Physiological Reviews, 100(3), 1181–1228. https://doi.org/10.1152/physrev.00033.2019

Choo, Y. J., Boudier-Revéret, M., & Chang, M. C. (2020). The Essentials of Brain Anatomy for Physiatrists. American Journal of Physical Medicine & Rehabilitation, 100(2), 181–188. https://doi.org/10.1097/phm.0000000000001558

Thau. (2021, October 14). Anatomy, Central Nervous System. https://pubmed.ncbi.nlm.nih.gov/31194336/

Ackerman, S. (2022). Major Structures and Functions of the Brain. Nih.gov; National Academies Press (US). https://www.ncbi.nlm.nih.gov/books/NBK234157/

Domingos, C., Silva, C. M. da, Antunes, A., Prazeres, P., Esteves, I., & Rosa, A. C. (2021). The Influence of an Alpha Band Neurofeedback Training in Heart Rate Variability in Athletes. International Journal of Environmental Research and Public Health, 18(23), 12579. https://doi.org/10.3390/ijerph182312579

Reis, J., Portugal, A. M., Fernandes, L., Afonso, N., Pereira, M., Sousa, N., & Dias, N. S. (2016). An Alpha and Theta Intensive and Short Neurofeedback Protocol for Healthy Aging Working-Memory Training. Frontiers in Aging Neuroscience, 8. https://doi.org/10.3389/fnagi.2016.00157

Gruzelier, J. (2008). A theory of alpha/theta neurofeedback, creative performance enhancement, long distance functional connectivity and psychological integration. Cognitive Processing, 10(S1), 101–109. https://doi.org/10.1007/s10339-008-0248-5

Fox, D. J., Tharp, D. F., & Fox, L. C. (2005). Neurofeedback: An Alternative and Efficacious Treatment for Attention Deficit Hyperactivity Disorder. Applied Psychophysiology and Biofeedback, 30(4), 365–373. https://doi.org/10.1007/s10484-005-8422-3

Enriquez-Geppert, S., Smit, D., Pimenta, M. G., & Arns, M. (2019). Neurofeedback as a Treatment Intervention in ADHD: Current Evidence and Practice. Current Psychiatry Reports, 21(6). https://doi.org/10.1007/s11920-019-1021-4

Veilahti, A. V. P., Kovarskis, L., & Cowley, B. U. (2021). Neurofeedback Learning Is Skill Acquisition but Does Not Guarantee Treatment Benefit: Continuous-Time Analysis of Learning-Curves From a Clinical Trial for ADHD. Frontiers in Human Neuroscience, 15. https://doi.org/10.3389/fnhum.2021.668780

Schönenberg, M., Wiedemann, E., Schneidt, A., Scheeff, J., Logemann, A., Keune, P. M., & Hautzinger, M. (2017). Neurofeedback, sham neurofeedback, and cognitive-behavioural group therapy in adults with attention-deficit hyperactivity disorder: a triple-blind, randomised, controlled trial. The Lancet Psychiatry, 4(9), 673–684. https://doi.org/10.1016/s2215-0366(17)30291-2

Marzbani, H., Marateb, H., & Mansourian, M. (2016). Methodological Note: Neurofeedback: A Comprehensive Review on System Design, Methodology and Clinical Applications. Basic and Clinical Neuroscience Journal, 7(2). https://doi.org/10.15412/j.bcn.03070208

About the Author

Jean-Maurice Cecilia-Menzel is an alternative practitioner of psychotherapy and a trained neurofeedback therapist. A three-year degree in health and social care, two years of training in psychotherapeutic work and ongoing research round off his career to date. He practices as an alternative practitioner of psychotherapy in his own office in Munich.

Read more at https://www.neurofeedback-praxis-muenchen.de.